INFORMATION MANAGEMENT USING dBASE

A. NEIL YERKEY

NEAL-SCHUMAN PUBLISHERS, INC.
NEW YORK   LONDON

Published by Neal-Schuman Publishers, Inc.
100 Varick Street
New York, NY 10013

Printed and bound in the United States of America

Library of Congress Cataloging-in-Publication Data

Yerkey, A. Neil.
    Information management using dBASE / by A. Neil Yerkey.
        p.   cm.
    Includes bibliographical references and index.
    ISBN 1-55570-094-2
    1. Libraries--Automation--Computer programs. 2. Microcomputers-
-Library applications. 3. dBase III plus (Computer program)
4. dBase IV (Computer program) 5. Information technology.
I. Title.
Z678.93.D33Y47 1991
025.3'0285'536--dc20   91-28220
                                                CIP

Contents

Part 1. Using Computers for Information Management

Part 2. dBASE Serials System Application

List of Programs

List of Figures

Introduction

DATA AND INFORMATION

Information Management Using dBASE is a book about information. Although I agree with Charles Bernier that information is ultimately a change in the central nervous system, I will adopt the more popular idea that information is raw data organized in ways that make it useful to someone.[1] Computers process data and produce information. Data are the raw materials, the bits and pieces of "signals that indicate that an event has taken place."[2] As your computer arranges, relates, summarizes, sorts, and classifies those pieces of raw data, they become more and more meaningful and gradually become information that you can use. *Information Management Using dBASE* is about how computers can rearrange and relate those pieces of raw data into useful patterns of information to meet specific needs.

The modern world is becoming increasingly dependent on the creation, use, and communication of information for economic and social well-being. We live in a data-rich society with more data being created and made available to more people than ever before. But to make informed decisions does not necessarily require more data. Instead, decision makers need data that is transformed into meaningful patterns of information. Microcomputers are powerful tools that facilitate this transformation.

We, as information professionals, must be careful to develop people-oriented systems for managing and retrieving this data and information. That is, data must be patterned into information that meets specific demands of people in specific circumstances.

INFORMATION MANAGEMENT IN LIBRARIES

What is information management? According to Shelly and Cashman, information management is:

> The task of managing and controlling the data and information required within an organization for that organization to function.[3]

What data and information must libraries manage for them to function? We who work in libraries and information handling agencies are up to our metaphorical necks in information processing activities, whether or not we use computers. Information professionals have always faced two kinds of tasks that require information management: managing the collection and managing the library's financial and personnel resources.

Managing the Collection

This is the stuff of libraries. It includes keeping track of reference books, indexes, and abstracts, magazines, government documents, handbooks, and on and on. Most of these materials are "prepackaged," and come into the library ready and able to answer questions, provide material for term papers, solve problems, or provide recreation. With the use of a microcomputer database these data may be organized to retrieve this information. For example, a reference librarian may create a database to search for titles of reference books to answer specific types of questions; in a corporate library, a database could organize relevant indexes in relation to their subject and journal coverage; a data management system could assist in serials control by keeping account of both available and missing newspapers and journals.

Libraries are also inundated with thousands of information-bearing pieces of paper and other media that are not prepackaged. Databases can be used to make vertical files, local educational and cultural information, or employment opportunities accessible to the library's clientele. Databases can also be created to provide unique subject access to collections in special libraries.

Managing Resources

Libraries are complex organizations, sometimes with budgets in the millions of dollars. They are also labor intensive, relying on efficient use of professional, clerical, and student staff. The principles of information management can be applied in dozens of ways in this environment:

- Personnel management
- Staffing and scheduling
- Budgeting and financial management
- Community relations
- Resource management
- AV equipment inventory
- Acquisition information
- Project management
- Interlibrary loan
- Film/slides booking systems

- Supplies inventory control
- Skills inventory
- Various membership projects (e.g., Friends of the Library).

The tasks of managing the collection and managing resources often overlap. I will use a Serials Control and Information System (hereafter called Serials System) to show how to use a database to organize information relevant to both tasks, as well as to illustrate some information management ideas. These illustrations should be applicable to other library activities as well, such as circulation control, or acquisitions and technical processing.

HOW TO USE THIS BOOK

Information Management Using dBASE will look at how computers work in the storage, management, retrieval, and manipulation of data, and how they produce relevant information. It is not concerned with hardware such as disk drives, modems, printers, or monitors. It is written for the person who knows something about microcomputers but wishes to learn more about how to manage information effectively. It is also written for the person who may already know something about dBASE[4] but who wishes to learn how to apply it to library applications, or how to use it more effectively in any setting.

dBASE III+ and dBASE IV are powerful, flexible systems, rich in commands and options. Sometimes there are several ways of doing the same thing, and the options often present a bewildering array of choices for the system designer. I hope to provide insight into why and when to choose one way of doing things over another, why and when to use different methods to organize, search, relate, put data into, and display data from, databases.

Part 1 describes information processing in general terms: how computers work and what they do to change data into information. Chapters 1 and 2 cover some very basic computer concepts and chapter 3 relates these concepts specifically to databases. A reader already familiar with these ideas may wish to skip Part 1. Part 2 describes how to use dBASE in a library serials control application. The emphasis in Part 2 is on dBASE III+ because it has almost become the de facto standard among relational databases. I hasten to add that the many enhancements in dBASE IV should not be minimized. It is a very powerful and flexible system, and learning to use it would be beneficial. I have emphasized dBASE III+ for three reasons: for now, dBASE III+ is more widely available in libraries; there is far more software available to use in conjunction with dBASE III+; and most important, everything you learn from this book about III+ will work with IV, but not the other way around. I will discuss significant enhancements in IV throughout the book.

Here is a summary of what each chapter covers:

Chapter 1 is an introduction to microcomputers and the way they handle data. It describes what computers do. how they do it, and how RAM, ROM, the CPU and hardware interact. A general discussion of programs and programming languages sets the stage for a more specific examination in later chapters.

Chapter 2 focuses on files, building from the smallest element, a data bit, to larger groupings of fields and records. It examines different methods of organizing, accessing, and relating files, and shows the advantages and disadvantages of each method.

Chapter 3 describes databases and analyzes different database models. It sets forth some necessary rules for database design.

Chapter 4 introduces the Serials Control System that will be used throughout the rest of the book to illustrate dBASE techniques.

Chapter 5 describes dBASE files specifically and introduces the files used by the Serials System. It shows the best ways to create dBASE database files.

Chapter 6 is an introduction to dBASE programming. It tells how to write programs using dBASE and goes into the various parts of dBASE programming commands.

Chapter 7 describes in more detail some useful functions and programming commands that are used throughout the sample programs.

Chapter 8 presents techniques for designing screens to input data. Here, specific programming commands relating to screen design and data input are examined.

Chapter 9 describes techniques for sorting and indexing databases, and explains how to use each method, and when.

Chapter 10 focuses on commands and options available to relate files. Relating several files makes the most of a relational database, and this chapter discusses the advantages and disadvantages of several options.

Chapter 11 goes into detail about the options for searching a database and presenting information to the user. It also discusses how to delete data safely.

Chapter 12 shows how to put the various parts together to make a working whole. It describes menus, subprograms, validity checks, error traps, compiling, and other techniques that make a reliable, stand-alone system.

Chapter 13 gives examples of other library applications, including using dBASE for Boolean subject searches.

No single book can cover everything about microcomputers, or even library applications of microcomputers. You are encouraged to consult the books in the bibliography for a deeper understanding of specific aspects of information processing.

Endnotes

1. See the following discussions concerning the problems of defining information: C. Bernier and A. N. Yerkey, *Cogent Communication* (Westport, Conn.: Greenwood Press, 1979) 18-19; K.J. McGarry. *The Changing Context of Information; An Introductory Analysis* (London: Bingley, 1981); Norman Stevens, "The History of Information, in *Advances in Librarianship*," Vol. 14 (Orlando, Fla.: Academic Press, 1986) 1-48.
2. William L. Harrison. *Computers and Information Processing* (St. Paul: West Publishing Co., 1985) 14.
3. Gary Shelly and Thomas Cashman. *Computer Fundamentals for an Information Age* (Brea, Calif.: Anaheim Publishing Co., 1984).
4. dBASE, dBASE III, dBASE III Plus (often abbreviated dBASE III+), and dBASE IV are registered trademarks of Ashton-Tate, Torrance, Calif. Unless otherwise noted, references to dBASE will be to dBASE III Plus.

Part 1
Using Computers For Information Management

1

Introduction To The Computer

In this chapter I will set the stage for information management by looking at some fundamentals of computer storage, types of software, and the interaction of software with the computer.

WHAT DO COMPUTERS DO?

Figure 1.1 is a schematic diagram of the computer. It has a PROCESSOR and two kinds of memory: read-only memory (ROM), which contains built-in programs, and random-access memory (RAM), which temporarily stores other programs and data during processing. These three components work together to process data into meaningful information.

The computer accepts data from a variety of INPUT devices such as keyboards, scanners, telephone lines, other computers, and barcode wands. This is the way to get data from the outside world into memory for processing.

All the processing is done under the direction of one or more PROGRAMS. The programs and some data must be loaded into RAM from a DISK before any useful work can be done.

OUTPUT devices such as video screen displays, printers, microfilm, telephone lines, and sound speakers, communicate the results. Output from one computer may become input to another.

FIGURE 1.1 Schematic of the Computer

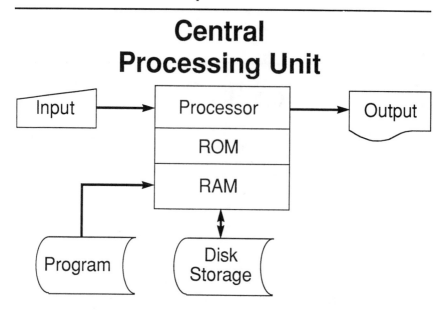

GETTING FROM DATA TO INFORMATION

Burch identifies several processing steps which convert data into information[1]. Dunikoski and Mandell[2] place the steps into the framework of Figure 1.1. They are:

Input

- Capturing—recording data from an event or occurrence.
- Verifying—checking and validating data to insure they were captured properly.
- Coding—converting the data from human form to machine-readable form.

Processing

- Classifying—placing data elements into specific categories.
- Arranging—placing data elements into specified sequences.
- Summarizing—combining and aggregating data either mathematically or in some logical way.
- Calculating—arithmetic and/or logical manipulation of data.

Output

- Reproducing—moving data from one medium to another, usually from memory to a printer, from memory to the screen, or from one disk to another.
- Disseminating—transferring data from one place to another.

Storage

- Storing—placing data on some storage medium such as disks.
- Retrieving—searching out specific data.

MILLIONS OF SWITCHES

The computer is nothing but a bunch of switches, millions of them, all wired together. In the earliest, experimental days, these were actual, physical switches, or relays. Soon, the vacuum tube, and later the transistor, performed the switching duties. Today, integrated circuits (ICs), or chips, contain thousand of invisible, silent, and incredibly fast switches. They perform their switching functions chemically and electronically instead of physically, like light switches. More accurately, they are "gates," allowing or stopping current flow.

The computer has a way to tell whether a particular gate is open or closed, and the patterns of opened and closed gates represent data in a computer. Setting a switch and sensing how it is set is a way of storing data. It is memory. Data can be stored, "remembered," moved around, and reported upon by sensing the way the switches are set and reset.

THE PROCESSOR CHIP: THE MAIN GATE

One of these integrated circuits is called the processor chip. The processor is the brains of the computer; the computer's computer. The computer either moves all instructions and data into the processor chip for processing, or else it places instructions there telling it where to find the data. (Actually, nothing is "moved," "placed," "written," or "read." Switches are set and sensed to represent the presence of data. For example, "moving" data means setting switches in one part of memory to duplicate it in another part. It is impossible to avoid metaphors when discussing data processing.) This chip does the arithmetic, comparing, fetching, putting, changing, and all the other operations necessary to process data.

Much of the evolution of microcomputers has centered on the evolution of the processor chip. They have names like Z80, 8088, 80386,

68000, and so on. Computers are said to be "based" on a chip. It is not surprising that computer buffs, given the way they enjoy using jargon, talk about computers as if the brand name of the computer is the name of the processor. You will hear people say: "That is my 386 computer, it is faster than the old Z80 I used to have." This means: "This computer with an Intel 80386 processor is faster than an older one that used a Zilog Z80 processor."

Many older computers were built around the Z80 chip manufactured by Zilog. It almost became the standard. But Apple computers used a Motorola 6502 chip, making for a total lack of compatibility between Apple and Z80 computers. A few other manufacturers used other chips, further confusing the situation.

Most of the chips in the 1970s, including the Z80, were 8 bit processors. They processed data and instructions 8 bits at a time. An 8 bit processor has some characteristics that limited the use of microcomputers. One is the maximum internal storage capacity. An 8 bit processor can handle memory size of about 65,000 bytes or characters (see the section below on RAM). This is not enough for many applications.

The other problem is that they are relatively slow, especially for "processor-intensive" activities like doing arithmetic, creating graphics, and comparing and changing large amounts of data. They are also "single-task" processors, meaning they can handle only one program at a time.

In 1981 IBM introduced its PC running on an Intel 8088 chip. This was a 16 bit chip that ran in an 8 bit mode, in hopes it would be compatibile with older machines. Fat chance; it eventually made older machines obsolete! It did have the advantage of allowing one million characters to be stored in internal memory, a great increase from the 65,000 limit of the Z80 machines. It also ran a bit faster.

IBM upgraded the PC in 1984. The new machine was based on the Intel 80286 chip. This chip can address millions of bytes of memory. It was also capable of multitasking. Multitasking allows several jobs to run on the computer simultaneously. Multitasking requires enormous amounts of memory, high speed, and most importantly, a chip which can partition memory and protect one job from another.

Recently, chips have been developed that process 32 bits at a time. The Intel 80386 chip is much faster, addresses more memory, and permits multitasking. It can work as one powerful 32 bit processor or as several 8086 processors operating simultaneously, almost like having several computers in one box.

Meanwhile, Apple stayed with the Motorola 68000 family of processors for its Macintosh computers. The Macintosh and IBM operate on very different design philosophies. It is almost as if the Mac is "right brained" and IBM is "left brained":

[Macintoshes are] intuitive, graphic-centered machines [which] invite exploration and play . . . . [IBM computers] like things articulated. . . . They are alphanumeric, stoic, project-oriented.[3]

The Macintosh is marvelous for many things, especially desk-top publishing and user-friendly multitasking. IBM PC/XT/AT/PS2 machines are stronger at organizing and managing large amounts of information. This book will concentrate on the IBM family, its clones, and "work-alikes."

ROM: BUILT-IN PROGRAMS

A particular grouping of ICs is called ROM. These are permanently set gates (hence, they are "read only memory"). Manufacturers preprogram them to do certain things, mostly to control input and output, monitor the status of the computer at different times, get it started when first turned on, and the like. These programs cannot be changed, and they are always there even when you turn the computer off.

RAM: WHERE IT ALL GOES

A large set of ICs is called RAM (a more descriptive acronym would be RAWM for "read and write memory"). RAM is the internal storage location of the computer. It is temporary storage, not suitable for storing data and information except for the brief time they are being processed. More permanent storage requires an external medium such as a disk. All data and programs go into and come from RAM during processing.

Three important characteristics of RAM are:

- It is *destructive read-in*. This means that when you (or, more accurately, your program) place data into RAM, you destroy any data already stored at the same location (the switches are reset).
- It is *nondestructive read-out*. Data can be sensed, reported on, and moved to another location without destroying the original. When your program moves data from one memory location to another it is really copying it in the new location.
- It is *volatile*. Data remain in memory only while power is applied. If you turn off the computer, even for a split second, you wipe out all data in RAM (unless you have constant battery power or a battery backup power supply). So, you must store data and programs permanently on some external device, usually disks.

ASCII Codes

The computer stores letters of the alphabet, punctuation, special characters, and numbers not used for calculation as patterns of 0s and 1s using a scheme called the American Standard Code for Information Interchange (ASCII). For example, the letter "A" is stored in memory as 01000001, the letter "B" as 01000010, "C" as 01000011, and so on. Upper- and lower-case letter pairs have entirely different bit patterns—the letter "a" is 01100001. The numeral "2" is 00110010. Notice that this is 2 as a *character*, not the number. Numerals represented in ASCII are *display characters*, not integers; you do not normally do arithmetic with these characters. Numbers used for arithmetic are stored and represented differently.

The ASCII code also includes patterns that represent things like carriage return, tab, and cursor movement. These are called *control codes*. Control codes apply to display devices like monitors and printers. For example, when I finish this paragraph and hit the carriage return, my word processed document will contain a 00001101 at the end of this line, representing a carriage return.

ASCII Values

Some information management activities make use of these values. They are used to alphabetize and make conditional comparisons for decision making. Unfortunately, upper case "Z" comes before (has a lower number) than lower case "a." Numerals come before letters. Some punctuation marks have lower values than letters and some have higher values.

This makes for strange alphabetization, a cause of concern among librarians. If you or I had designed the ASCII scheme, we would have given lower case letters immediately higher numbers than their upper case counterparts, so that "A" and "a" would alphabetize together. The codes were developed when computers only used upper case characters, so the lower case letters were appended rather than integrated.

Since an 8 bit code can represent 256 different characters, the standard ASCII codes leave many patterns unused. Computer manufacturers have extended the standard code to include special symbols like smiling faces, hearts, diamonds, foreign characters, and the like. These are not available on all microcomputers and their values are not standard.

Different computers may use different coding schemes, but it all boils down to setting groups of integrated circuit switches on and off in patterns recognized as having some meaning by the computer and its peripherals like printers, modems, and other computers. If two computers use different coding schemes, it becomes very difficult for them to share data.

PROGRAMMING AND PROGRAM LANGUAGES

The computer is useless without programs to tell it what to do. A program is a set of step-by-step instructions that tell the computer how to work on data. ROM contains some programs, but most are external to the hardware and must be loaded (brought in) from disks to RAM when needed.

Kinds of Programs—By Function

Programs may be classified in several overlapping ways. One classification is according to function:

Operating System Programs.
These are specialized programs that interpret the commands which operate the computer. All other programs work through the operating system to facilitate input and output, file management, reading and writing to disks, copying programs and disks, and the like. The most commonly used operating system for IBM compatible machines is MS-DOS, which stands for Microsoft (Corporation) Disk Operating System. Newer IBM's also use an operating system called OS/2.

DOS performs three main functions. The first function is as a *master program*, providing an interface between the peripheral devices and memory, controlling the allocation of memory, and trying to get programs to behave. The second DOS function is as *program manager*. This part loads and runs your programs.

The third function is the most visible. It is the *command interpreter*. The operating system allows you to control many activities on the computer directly, such as copying files, displaying directories, erasing files, setting or changing the date, displaying the contents of files, and so on. These are examples of operating system commands.

Commands differ from program instructions. Programs contain step-by-step instructions, which, taken together, perform some useful work. As an analogy, consider the military: direct commands from an officer to do this or that differ from battle plans drawn up at headquarters which instruct foot soldiers and officers alike how to take a parcel of ground. Operating system commands are direct commands to perform an immediate function. Programs are files of instructions to perform an application. Commands operate immediately; programs must be run.

When you type an operating system command such as DIR B:, the system consults an in-memory recipe book (a file called COM-MAND.COM) for the letters "DIR". The recipe book tells the computer what to do (in this case: "Turn on the disk drive labelled B, move the read-write head to track 20, read the directory which is located there, and put it on the screen").

Some command recipes, once loaded during booting, reside in memory and are always available. Others are, themselves, small programs which must be loaded into memory and run. The former are called resident or internal commands; the latter are variously called transient, external, or nonresident. If the computer does not find the command in memory, it loads a program which has the same name as the command and follows its instructions.

Utility Programs.
These are special-purpose programs to make the computer easier to use: programs to look into memory, help with debugging and development of programs, repair damaged disks, and so on.

Applications Programs.
These are programs that do useful work: spreadsheets, database man-agement programs, word processing programs, and the hundreds of other programs that turn the computer into a useful tool.

Kinds of Programs: By Level

Another way to classify programs is according to level. The word has at least two meanings:

1. In terms of "distance" from the hardware—higher level programs have more intervening programs between them and the hardware.
2. In terms of the language—program languages that are more English-like are higher level than those that are more machine-like. The meanings overlap and are intertwined, and cannot be analyzed sepa-rately. What follows is my attempt to integrate the two.

Distance Levels.
The lowest level are those programs that directly interact with the machine. These are the programs that are permanently "etched" into ROM. In the IBM PC they are called BIOS for Basic Input Output System (this has nothing to do with the BASIC language). BIOS are built-in, permanent programs for operating the hardware, the disk drives, monitors, keyboard, printers, and modems. They "awaken" the computer and perform various hardware initialization, including check-

ing RAM to make sure it is OK. With very few exceptions, all programs go through ROM to get things done.

When you boot the computer, a ROM program loads a single program from a disk. ROM is only smart enough to load one program, and it must physically be at one designated place on the disk. This second program, which is much smarter, takes over and loads other even smarter programs that make up DOS. Once the computer loads DOS, it is ready to go. The operating system is a step removed from ROM and the hardware.

In terms of distance from the hardware, applications programs and utilities that work through the operating system are at the highest program level. A "well behaved" program works through the operating system and lets the operating system work through ROM and the hardware. The higher level programs leave the hardware alone.

Language Levels.

Programs in ROM are electronic, that is, they are integrated circuits whose gates have been permanently set. They are "very low level," being far removed from English. The operating system and all other working programs are in machine language, a little higher than integrated circuits but also not very much like English. You should understand that *all* programs, regardless of their distance level, operate at the machine-language level.

However, not all programs are originally *written* in machine language (in fact, few are). Ultimately, all must be *translated* into machine language since that is the only language the computer understands. Most applications programs are sold as machine language programs. They come as files on disks, which, when read into memory, set the RAM switches in ways that the computer can interpret as instructions.

High level languages, such as BASIC, COBOL, PASCAL, and C, are best for program development. These allow the programmer to concentrate on the problem instead of the computer. The instructions are more like English and not so difficult to learn. In addition, high level languages are not specific to one machine or class of machines. Although BASIC has many dialects, it is similar across different models of computers; COBOL is even more standardized.

dBASE is a machine language programming system that contains a high level development language. You can use dBASE as it comes out of the box, or write your own custom programs with it.

INTERPRETERS

Some programs, most notably those written in BASIC or dBASE, remain in the high level language and are interpreted or translated into machine language *while they are being run*. There is a program to do this called an interpreter that must be loaded into memory before the program can be executed. The interpreter translates each instruction into machine language just before the computer executes it.

The interpreter must translate the high level program anew *each time* it is run—interpretation is temporary. Interpreters are best used during program development but they are not satisfactory for serious applications for the following reasons:

- Interpreted languages are slow. The computer must analyze each program instruction, look up the wording in the interpreter's dictionary, check it for errors, and translate it into machine language. It must do this each time the statement is "hit" and this could be dozens or hundreds of times during normal processing. This slows execution.
- Interpreted programs must have the interpreter present to run. This means that the user must have a copy of the interpreter and know how to use it. He or she must begin and end with the interpreter. Interpreted programs do not "stand alone."
- The interpreter checks statements for errors only when the statement is executed. In a complex set of programs some statements may not be properly checked before the programs are released for use. Then, when it is least expected, the program goes down a path it never went down before and, behold, an error!

COMPILERS

Another method is to translate once and for all—that is, translate each instruction ahead of time and store the translated instructions as a machine language version of the program. A translator program called a compiler does this. The machine language version is the one that is executed. Most commercial programs have been compiled.

Compiling takes more time initially than interpreting, but it only needs to be done once (assuming the program works as anticipated). Compiled programs run *much* faster than interpreted ones. Another advantage is that compiling checks the entire program for errors (they will not compile if there are errors).

The most compelling advantage of compiling is that it creates a stand-alone, executable, program. The user of a compiled program does not need to own the language in which it was developed. In other words, a compiled BASIC or dBASE program does not need BASIC or dBASE to run. It is not worth compiling a simple program that you seldom use, but may be very much worth compiling serious, heavily used programs.

dBASE is an interpreted language although separate compilers are available for it. I discuss dBASE compilers in Chapter 12.

ASSEMBLERS

Some programs are developed in an intermediate-level language called assembly language. It is not English-like but is easier to work with than machine language. Assembly language programs must be translated into machine language by a program called an assembler.

FIGURE 1.2   Program Levels

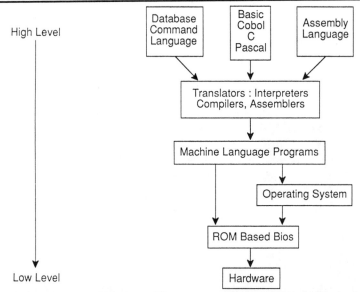

If all this business about levels and interaction of multiple programs is confusing, just remember that computers are totally stupid. Everything they do, a program must tell them how to do it. Therefore, several programs are interacting with each other all the time. Figure 1.2 illustrates program levels. In the center of the diagram is a box labelled TRANSLATORS. All programs must be sent through a translator (either an interpreter or compiler) to be converted into machine language. The relative level of programs *above* this box depends on how English-like they are. Programs *below* the TRANSLATOR box are always in machine language. The number of steps away from the hardware determines the relative level of these. It is at the hardware level that things get done.

Endnotes

1. John Burch, Felix Strater, and Gary Grudnitski. *Information System: Theory and Practice* 5th ed. (New York: Wiley, 1989).
2. Robert Dunikoski and Steven Mandell. *Computers and Information Processing Today* (St. Paul: West Publishing Co., 1986).
3. Lawrence Magid and Marty Jerome, "IBM vs. Apple," *PC/Computing* August, 1988): 70-77

2

Computer Files

Files are at the heart of information management. Even if you know nothing about RAM, ROM, DOS, and integrated circuits (it is not a bad idea to know something about these things), you must have a clear understanding of files to design a data management system. We will build our understanding from the smallest element, a bit, to the structure called a file. Later, I will extend the idea to the largest structure, a database, and finally to dBASE databases.

GROUPS OF DATA

We group things to help us come to grips with the complexities of life. Grouping, classifying, and abstracting help us see the relatedness of things which might get away if isolated. This is structure. Computers do not automatically group things, but the computer is a useful tool to help us form groupings. Our ideas about fields, records, and files are human ideas, not computer ones. When people first began to use the computer, they organized their data as it was in pre-computer days. Just as the first automobiles resembled familiar carriages, the first record structures resembled card files, address books, file folders, and so on. These metaphors formed the basis of computer literacy and still persist.

It soon became evident that computers could manage without these pre-computer structures so scientists developed new structures that make better use of the computer's capabilities. We are in the midst of a structural transition. Many programmers, programming languages, and data management software use the older field/record/file structure. Others use newer structures that do away with the idea of fields and records altogether. I will stick with the field/record/file ideas because dBASE uses them.

BYTES AND CHARACTERS

The computer stores data, whether in memory or on files, in or on something existing in one of two states. As we have seen, one bit in RAM is a gate turned on or off within an integrated circuit. In files, it is the absence or presence of a magnetized spot on some medium like a disk surface.

Except to computer buffs, bits do not mean much, so we group several bits into patterns representing characters. We call one grouping of several bits a byte. The word *byte* is not very precise. Traditionally (as traditional as you can get in the short history of microcomputers), a byte is eight bits arranged in a pattern to represent one character—a letter of the alphabet, a punctuation mark, a special symbol.

One character's worth of data is the lowest level of structure: groupings of bits turned on and off to represent data. The word OHIO is a "string" of four characters, or bytes, each of which is represented by eight bits, turned on and off in different patterns. Ohio looks like this:

```
01001111011010000110100101001111
O       H       I       O
```

There is nothing magical about 01001111 representing the letter O. It is just another instance of using the American Standard Code for Information Interchange (ASCII) to represent characters.

DATA ELEMENTS AND FIELDS

Data elements are pieces of information provided as input or produced as output by the computer. The phrase is not used consistently. Sometimes it is synonymous with field, sometimes it is used to mean the individual words of data that make up a field. I will define a data element as the smallest unit of information that is meaningful to humans. A field may consist of one data element, or it may be made up of several.

For example, words like Ohio or Smith are data elements. So are "words" like 32 (an age), 36789 (a salary), or M (as in male or female). Phrases like Akron, Ohio or John Smith are two data elements each, although we sometimes think of phrases like these as single data elements.

Normally, the I in OHIO is not a data element. It is a character. However, a single letter may sometimes be a very meaningful data element. For example, the letter M may carry as much meaning as the word male. So, a data element is something that means something to someone.

It is necessary to distinguish between the contents of a field and its name. The field's contents are known as its value. The value might be Mary Smith, Acoustical Society of America, or Dubuque, Iowa. The name of the field is what it is called. It is a name given by you to move data into or out of a file. The above three values might go into fields called NAME, PUBLISHER, CITY-STATE; or they might go into AAA, BBB, CCC. The field name remains the same from record to record; the field values change from record to record.

The phrase Akron, Ohio might be the value of a single CITY-STATE field made up of two data elements. Add another data element, 44312, to make it CITY-STATE-ZIP field. Add an address, 67 Countryside Lane, and make the whole thing an ADDRESS field.

Now we have a problem: where does a data element stop and a field begin? Good question. In Figure 2.1 (a) all data are lumped into one field called ADDRESS. This is not very useful for retrieval of specific elements. To make it more useful, the data could be broken into two fields, STREET and CITY-STATE as in (b), or each element could be placed into a separate field, as in (c).

FIGURE 2-1   Contents of Fields

NUMBER OF FIELDS PER RECORD	NAME OF FIELD	CONTENTS OF FIELD
(a) One Field	ADDRESS	672 Martin Rd, Akron, Ohio, 44312
(b) Two Fields	STREET CITYSTATE	672 Martin Rd Akron, Ohio 44312
(c) Four Fields	STREET CITY STATE ZIP	672 Martin Rd Akron Ohio 44312

Which to use? The decision rests with you, the file designer, depending on what you expect to do with the data. The first design is simple to put data into but you will have trouble sorting, retrieving, comparing, classifying, or selecting data from it. Input is simple but output is restricted. It falls into the category of "free text." The third design is the most complex for putting data in, but the most flexible for getting it out.

Fields are the most natural units for sorting, searching, retrieving, printing, or displaying. You would have a hard time sorting on or retrieving by the city in Figure 2.1(a), but put the city into a field of its own and you have a hook with which to grab it.

RECORDS AND FILES

Fields are grouped into records. A record is data about one thing: one person, one book, one employee, one piece of AV equipment, and so on. Every record in a file is about a different constituent of the same population. Whereas fields have names, records do not.

Although you search or sort by *fields*, what you display or move around are *records*. If you search the CITY field for "Buffalo," you will retrieve all the records that have that value in the CITY field.

A file is a named collection of related records. It is a gathering of records as they relate to one environment: a personnel file, a bibliographic file, a sales file, an equipment inventory file.

Files are named and stored on disks. Each file on a disk (or subdirectory of a disk) must have a unique name. In MS DOS, the name may consist of two parts: the required filename of from one to eight characters, and an optional extension, separated by a period.

We have been building data into increasingly meaningful groups of information. Bits are individual magnetized spots. Bytes are groupings of bits to represent characters. Characters are put together into data elements, data elements into fields, fields into records, and records into files. What is the next grouping? Groups of files into databases? Yes, but not always. We will see why in the next chapter.

FILE ORGANIZATION AND ACCESS

There are two related, but separate, ideas surrounding disk storage: file organization and file access. File access refers to the way the computer finds and retrieves records from the file. File organization refers to the way the computer puts data on files; that is, the way records are organized relative to each other.

Although there are several types of storage media, I will assume here that data are being stored on disks. Also, dBASE uses a unique file structure and a separate chapter will be devoted to dBASE files.

Most books on microcomputers consider just two kinds of files: *sequential* and *random*. These words refer to the file's organization type. But random files may be accessed randomly or sequentially, so a distinction should be made between access and organization.

File Access

Specifically, access refers to whether you retrieve records from the file in the same order as put on or in a more random order. There are two kinds of access:

Sequential access means that you read records from the file from the beginning to the end. Any file may be accessed sequentially, despite how they were created or their organization type.

Random access, more accurately called direct access, means that you read records from the file in an order different from the physical order of the records. In other words, you may read record 4 first, then record 2, then record 124. To do random access, you must create a file as a random file. This brings me to file organization.

File Organization

File organization has to do with the order of the records (where each record is placed in relation to other records), and how the computer knows where records stop and start.

Sequential Organization

In the microcomputer environment, a sequential file is one in which data are placed on the file one "record" after another, with a marker or delimiter between each record. A "record" is the data between two delimiters, not necessarily a record as defined earlier. Each access to the file brings in the data between two of these delimiters.

When the computer, driven by a program, reads from a sequential file, it does not know about fields, records, names, addresses, or telephone numbers. It just brings in the next set of data and stops when it hits the delimiter. The *program* gives structure to the data being read in. The programmer assigns the incoming data to variables that represent names, addresses, telephone numbers, salaries, and so on. The file just has a series of data elements separated by delimiters. See Figure 2.2, in which delimiters are represented by commas.

FIGURE 2.2   Sequential File Organization

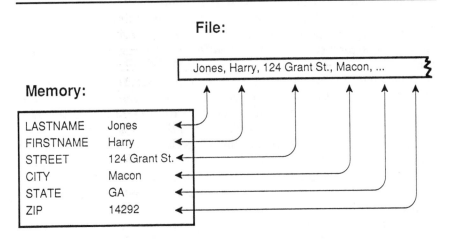

Incidentally, the BASIC language makes extensive use of sequential files. Field names reside in the program, not on the file. Later, we will see how this differs from dBASE files.

An advantage of sequential files is that they are simple to create, understand, and use. Other kinds of file organizations require more complex programming. They also save space by using variable length records. For example, one serial title may be *Byte* while another may be *Journal of the American Society for International Governmental Relations*. Each of these names will take up only as much space on a sequential file as it needs. This is not so with other file types that may require a short title like BYTE to take as much space as the longest title.

The major disadvantage of sequential files is the inability to read records randomly. If you need the title of the 20th record you must read past the first 19. Worse, you cannot easily back up and next read the 12th—sequential access of a sequential file must always start at the beginning of the file and go forward.

You may add records only to the *end* of a sequential file. And, you cannot insert into or delete from the middle without re-creating the entire file.

Random Organization

The disadvantages of sequential files sometimes outweigh their advantages, and most data management software uses random organization for their files and databases. A random file is one in which the location of records is determined by a relative record number (RRN).

Think of the file as strung-out mailboxes in an apartment building, each box holding the mail for one resident (one record), and each numbered from 1 to n (n being the number of residents). Whether the boxes have mail in them or not, they are numbered and take up space waiting for mail. If the resident in apartment #6 gets a letter, it goes into box #6; the next piece of mail coming in may be for box #150, next for #24, and so on. *The placing and removing of mail is based on the numbers assigned to each box, not on the order in which the mail was delivered.*

Likewise, the placement of records in a random file is based on a number that tells the computer into which "box" to put it. For example, the 12th record is the one addressed by a RRN of 12 and is the 12th record area, whether or not records exist in the first 11 areas.

For this to work, random files have fixed length records. This means that each record is the same length as every other record. Records have the same number of fields and the fields are the same length from record to record. Shorter data are padded with blanks and longer data are truncated to fit.

The computer can tell the beginning and end of a record because it knows that *each* record is so many bytes long. For this reason, random files seem to have normal field and record structures because the programmer must specify fields and field lengths for one record before putting the first record in the file.

For example, let us suppose that each record of a serials bibliography file is 116 bytes long. The computer will "know" that the second record (mailbox #2) begins 117 bytes from the beginning of the file, the fourth record begins at byte 465, and so on. To place a record on the file, retrieve a record, change, or delete a record, the program supplies the appropriate RRN. The system multiplies the RRN by the number of bytes in a record to know where in the file to find the desired record. See Figure 2.3.

Figure 2.3 Random File Organization

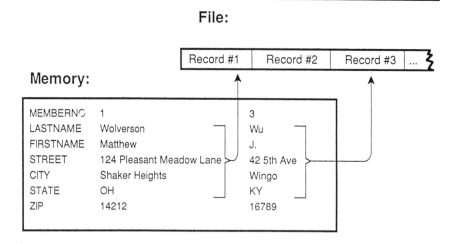

The obvious advantage of random files is that you may create and read the file in random order. You can jump around the file, backwards and forwards, reading records in any order. You also may add, delete, and change records in the middle of the file.

There are some disadvantages. Because you must specify the length of each field, *every* record will be the same length whether the data warrants it or not. This puts a burden on the programmer to decide the best length of each field. For example, 30 bytes for the serial title may be too short for some titles and too long for others. You must decide whether to truncate long titles or pad short ones (wasting file space), and it is difficult to change your mind once you have added data to the file.

Indexed Organization

Microcomputer programs rarely use true indexed files. True indexed files (sometimes called *indexed sequential*) are sequential files with internal indexes that allow records to be retrieved randomly.

For example, the serials bibliographic file might be arranged sequentially by ISSN with two internal indexes: one by TITLE and one by PUBLISHER. The file could then be accessed sequentially by ISSN, or randomly by title or publisher.

True indexed files maintain their internal indexes automatically; they do not have to be explicitly created or updated. Every time you add a new serial to the file, the title and publisher indexes will be updated.

Most microcomputer programs, including dBASE III+, use random files with one or more *separate* index files. You must create, maintain, and update the indexes separately each time you update the main file. dBASE IV uses a "multiple index file" which comes about as close as anything to true indexed files on a microcomputer; this option will be discussed in a later chapter.

3

Databases

In chapter 2, I defined fields as groupings of data elements, records as groupings of fields, and files as groupings of records. Would the next step be groupings of files into databases? Yes and no. A database is a grouping of files, but it is more than that. This chapter will discuss various ideas about databases and how they differ from merely a collection of files.

WHAT IS A DATABASE?

Here are four paraphrases that represent different ideas about databases:

1. *A collection of logically linked data files.* Here, the emphasis is on files. The files are "logically linked" or interrelated. A database may consist of two, ten, or twenty files, each containing some data. Specifically, some fields of a record may be in one file, some in another, and the complete record may be scattered across several files. In a serials database, for example, the title of a particular serial may be in one file, the publisher's name and address in another, and the subscription data in yet another. The emphasis is on files of data elements, instead of files of records.

2. *A collection of multiple records with built-in relationships between records and data items.* The emphasis here is on records, not files. This definition implies that files are not the responsibility of the data management system. They are physical objects—things that reside on disks and for which the operating system is responsible. The concern of the database management system is only with *records* that may be scattered all over the disk but bearing some kind of relationship to each other.

3. *A collection of related data.* This definition leaves out files and records altogether. Here, the emphasis is on data, not concerned with where and how the data are held together. The important thing is that bits and pieces of data are related in some way and that the management system can find needed pieces of data at the right time.
4. *An organized collection of related information or data.* This definition is from the *dBASE III+ Manual* and is really the definition of a *file*. dBASE confuses the database/file situation: files with fields and records are called databases in dBASE. On the other hand, dBASE can relate several files together, and it is the total collection of related files that usually make up a database. We simply must work around the confusion that results when dBASE gives the name database to both a single file and a collection of related files.

The important thing is that these definitions include the idea of *relatedness.* This is central to any ideas about databases. Beyond that, the definitions are very different. Some include the word "file," some do not; some include "record," some do not. How confusing! Can we put it together?

Part of the confusion is the result of thinking about a database from different viewpoints. For example, an analysis at the *file level* shows how files interrelate, how they are linked together, but an analysis at the *data level* focuses on the data, with no attempt to make *a-priori* interpretations of the data or the relationships between items. A hierarchical database is an example of a file level model and a relational database is an example of a data-level model[1]. A look at database models may clear up some of the confusion.

DATABASE MODELS: FLAT FILES

The simplest model (a single file) lacks interfile structure and is not really a database. I have included it here as a beginning point to draw the picture of relatedness. In this model, a single file contains all the data needed for an application. The data has one "view"—that which one specific application requires.

A few years ago, flat-file managers were mostly simple "card file" programs, suitable for only the simplest applications. Today, sophisticated flat-file managers are available. They are easy to use and may meet many data management needs.

A flat-file manager can sort, select, retrieve, report, and change data to meet different needs, but the data in one file cannot be related to data in other files. In short, flat files are simple but inflexible. They work well for simple data management tasks like mailing lists, but cannot meet the requirements of more sophisticated applications because the more sophisticated and complex the application, the less likely it is that you will be able to get all the data into just one file.

DATABASE MODELS: HIERARCHICAL

One way to relate data from several files is through a hierarchical model that organizes data like an upside-down tree (or an organization chart). The highest level is the "root," each lower level is a "node." The lowest set of nodes are sometimes called "leaves." That is the tree metaphor.

Another metaphor is of the family. The root is the parent (only one), each node is a child. Each child may have children.

Figure 3.1 is a pictorial representation of three files, each of which stores a portion of serials data (field names are shown instead of actual data, and the open rectangles hanging beneath represent records).

FIGURE 3.1   Hierarchical Database Model

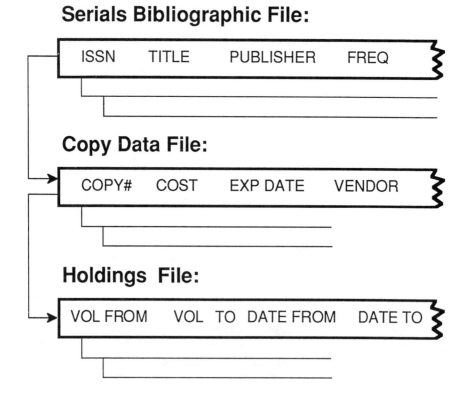

Serials Bibliographic File:

ISSN   TITLE   PUBLISHER   FREQ

Copy Data File:

COPY#   COST   EXP DATE   VENDOR

Holdings File:

VOL FROM   VOL TO DATE FROM   DATE TO

The Serials Bibliographic File contains bibliographic information about serials. There is one record for each serial that the library owns. This file is the "root." Subordinate to it is a Copy Data File. This file contains information about each copy that the library owns. Further subordinate is a Holdings File. There will be a separate record for each run of holdings for each copy. Holdings are "grandchildren" of the bibliographic data.

The library will own at least one, and possibly several, copies of each serial title in its collection. The record for each title will "point" (be related) to one or more copy records. Each copy will have one or more sets of check-in or holdings data, and a copy record may point to several records in the holdings file. To find the holdings for a particular serial you must start with the bibliographic data, go from there to a particular copy, and from there to the holdings for that copy.

Hierarchical models follow certain rules as described by Atre. Two are particularly important:

- Every record connects to one and only one record above it;
- Every record except the root must be accessed through its parent.

The first rule states that a parent may have several children but children may have only one parent (obviously not a biological model). The library may own several copies of a serial, but any one copy will be related to only one title. In other settings, a manager has several subordinates but each subordinate has only one manager; a surgeon has many patients but a patient has only one surgeon; the main library has several branches but each branch is part of only one main library. These are one-to-many relationships.

The second rule states that you need higher level data to give meaning to the whole. You must first access data on a high level to get data from a subordinate level. For example, to get a complete picture of a serial, you must start at the top, the bibliographic file, and work down to the holdings file.

Hierarchical models are best suited for data that naturally fits a hierarchical scheme: those based on one-to-many relationships. Unfortunately, this leaves out much real life data.

For example, data about students and their courses could not follow the first rule, since each course has several students and each student takes several courses. This is a many-to-many relationship, called a network.

DATABASE MODELS: NETWORKS

The network model fits more real life situations. It differs from the hierarchical in that a "child" may have more than one "parent" and a "parent" may have more than one "child." The students and courses example (Figure 3.2) uses two files. A Course File contains information about courses, and there will be one record for each course in the university. A Student File contains information about students. There will be one record for each student. A student may be enrolled in many courses and a course would contain many students. There is no inherent subordinate relationship, and, unlike the hierarchical model, the arrows have points on both ends. In terms of data access, you need not first obtain data about courses before finding data about students or vice versa. There is no "up" and "down." A node may be subordinate to another but not exclusively so. Linkages become vastly more complex but the network model is more flexible than the hierarchical model.

FIGURE 3.2 Network Database Model

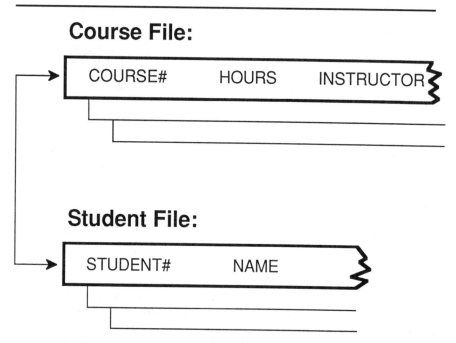

Course File:

COURSE#   HOURS   INSTRUCTOR

Student File:

STUDENT#   NAME

DATABASE MODELS: RELATIONAL

The emphasis in a relational model is on data more than files. It does not presuppose linkages. The data are cast as independent tables with linkages being made on an *ad hoc* basis as the need arises. It is as if you had several flat files with no hierarchical or network relationships inherent among them. The flat files stand alone until a database management system pulls them together as needed.

To illustrate this, consider data about course scheduling. There may be independent files (technically, these are called relations) about students, courses, teachers, classrooms, buildings, and class times. In any complex set of data, not everyone needs all the data all the time. One member of the administrative staff may need data about teachers and classrooms, another about students and courses, another about students, courses, and classrooms; another about classrooms, times, and buildings.

Nor are the data always needed in the same fixed, rigid ways. In July, a staff person may need some data elements but not others. In November, he or she may need yet another set. Data elements may be combined from several files in ways not even anticipated by the database designer.

It is awkward and probably impossible to access, update, relate, and keep secure if these data are all in one flat file. If the data were in several files with a hierarchical or network structure, the data linkages would be complex and hard to maintain.

A relational database offers the ability to get just what is needed, independently of what others need. Each user has his or her "view" of the data. Just the part he or she needs. The rest is there for others to use but relations are established from the data when and as needed.

The hierarchical model shown in Figure 3.1 may be recast as a relational model. All the data about serials may be spread across several files. One file may contain bibliographic data. A second file may contain data about copies. Others will contain data about publishers, vendors, or binding. The Acquisitions Department may need data about vendors. Public Services needs data about library holdings. Collection Development needs data about publishers, and so on.

Figures 3.3 through 3.5 and the discussion following illustrate the relational model. Data in a relational database are cast as one or more tables with rows and columns. Each row is one record, each column is a field, and the table is a file.[2] In these examples, the field names are shown at the top of each column, and sample data fills in the table. The computer does not *store* data in columns and rows; the table is just a way for us to understand relational data.

Figure 3.3 contains serials bibliographic data. A characteristics of a relational database is that "keys" link files together. Keys are one or more fields that uniquely identify a record. No two rows may have the same key value. In Figure 3.3 the ISSN is the key. It uniquely defines each serial title; no two titles have the same ISSN.

The file in Figure 3.4 contains data about each copy in the library, one row per copy. Since a library may have several copies of the same serial, the ISSN is not unique enough to serve as a key. A key may be made up of more than one field, so we combine ISSN with COPY (depicted as ISSN+COPY) to obtain a key that will uniquely identify each copy. Therefore, 0018-60821 differs from 0018-60822 (the last digit being the copy number).

FIGURE 3.3   Serials Bibliographic File

	Key		FIELDS		
	ISSN	TITLE	PUBLISHER	FREQ	..
R	0018-5868	Hospital Times	Western Hosp Assn	BW	
E	0018-6082	Hot Cars	Amer Hot Rod Assn	M	
C	1234-5678	Business Computing	Cahners	M	
O	0027-7134	NYLA Bulletin	New York Lib Assn	M	
R	0003-5491	Anthropology Quart	Catholic Univ	Q	
D	.	.	.	.	
S	.	.	.	.	

FIGURE 3.4   Serials Copy File

	Key			FIELDS			
	ISSN	COPY	COST	VENDOR	NOSVOL	VOLYR	..
R	0018-6082	1	25	M	12	2	
E	0018-6082	2	25	M	12	2	
C	1234-5678	1	15	F	12	1	
O	1234-5678	2	0	G	12	1	
R	0027-7134	1	50	D	12	4	
D	0003-5491	1	100	M	4	1	
S	.	.	.	.	.	.	

Figure 3.5 shows a table for the publisher's name and address. This data should be kept in a separate file. Notice that the key is PUB-

LISHER. Using this key, you can establish a relation between the
PUBLISHER field of the bibliographic file (Figure 3.3) and PUB-
LISHER of this one.

Figure 3.5 Publisher File

	Key		FIELDS		
	PUBLISHER	ADDRESS	CITY	STATE	..
R	Amer Hosp Assn	123 Grant St	Emporia	KA	
E	Selden Publ Co	45 Market St	Toledo	OH	
C	Ziff-Davis	1 Park Ave	New York	NY	
O	.	.	.	.	
R	.	.	.	.	
D	.	.	.	.	
S	.	.	.	.	

RULES FOR DATABASE DESIGN

Because we will be designing a relational database in Part II, we
must be aware of certain practical rules in database design. Technically,
we call these rules "normal forms," and the process of getting data ready
to go into a relational database is called "normalization."

You can design a database in a helter skelter fashion and possibly
get away with it. Everything will work—for awhile. These problems
develop when you add, delete, or update the data:

- Data will not go where you think it should go.
- When you remove unwanted data you are forced to remove wanted
  data.
- Simple additions become very complex.

You may not know anything about normal forms, but you will pay
for violating them. There are many rules, but the first three are most
important.

Rule 1 (First Normal Form)

This rule has two interrelated parts: The first task in getting data
ready for a relational database is to put them into a table with one row
for each record and one column for each field and a unique key for each

row. *If you cannot put your data into rows and columns, you cannot have a relational database.*

What this means in practical terms is that you cannot have a field that can take more than one value *per record.* For example, a book may have one author, one title, one publisher, but several subject headings. The subject headings cannot be in the same file (table) as the author and title. Try putting some books with several subject headings (but an unpredictable number) into a table with columns and rows, allowing only one row per book. It cannot be done if you do not know ahead of time how many subject headings any one book may have.

Let's take another example. A student has one name, one address, one student number, but he or she may take many courses and have many grades. A table can be drawn up containing the name, address, and student number, but courses and grades cannot be put into this table if limited to one line per student.

Where does the repeating data go? Into another file. For the book data, subjects go into a separate file. The thing that ties the files together is some common attribute, say the ISBN, which uniquely identifies each book. Each subject for each book becomes a separate record in the new database.

The student data would use two files: one containing the student's number, name, and address, and one containing the student's number, course number, and grade. See Figure 3.6.

For every course taken by every student, there will be a separate record (row) in the course file. This creates a little redundancy but it is the only way to have a relational database.

The second part of this rule states that each record must be unique—there can be no other record like it in the database—and one or more of the fields is designated as a key that uniquely identifies each record. Notice that the course file in Figure 3.6 uses STUDENT # plus COURSE # as the key. The student number is unique enough for the student's personal data, but not for the course data. Likewise, to identify a particular serial completely as it is held in a library, we must use the ISSN plus the copy number as the key.

The second part of the rule can be violated by dBASE. The dBASE management system does not require each record to be unique or even to have unique keys. Nonetheless, it is a good idea to follow this rule to prevent trouble down the road.

Rule 2 (Second Normal Form)

The second rule states that all fields must be identified by the *entire key.* This is only a problem when you have keys made up of more than one attribute (e.g., ISSN + Copy Number). Every other field must require the entire key, and not just part of it, for unique identification.

FIGURE 3.6   First Normal Form: Students and Courses

Student File:

┌─Key─┐

STUDENT #	NAME	ADDRESS	TELEPHONE	..
1234	James Smith	45 Block St	687-8876	
1346	Peter Jones	100 Disk Dr	876-3456	
8765	Mary Hart	789 Beaker St	432-1987	
.	.	.	.	

Course File:

┌─── Key ───┐

STUDENT #	COURSE #	GRADE
1234	LI598	B
7658	CS203	A
1234	LI500	A
1234	LI654	C
1346	MA223	A
.	.	.

The file in Figure 3.7(a) violates this rule (in the next few examples, I have omitted sample data and show only field names). The key is:BOOK # + BORROWER #. The problem is that the borrower's address has nothing to do with the book number. The name and address is only relevant to a portion of the key (BORROWER #).

Why is this a problem? If you want to find a borrower's name and address, you must know which books he or she has charged out! Worse, if you wish to change the borrower's address, you must scan through all the charge-out records and change every occurrence of it. The solution is to create a second file with BORROWER # as the key. The common BORROWER # ties the files together. See Figure 3.7(b).

Here, one file contains information about books charged out: which book, who has it, and the due date. A separate file contains information about the borrower. Notice that when the borrower returns a book, the record is removed from the charge-out file, *but the borrower file is undisturbed.* This way, you have a record of borrowers even if they have no books charged out. You can change the address without referring to the charge-out records.

FIGURE 3.7   Second Normal Form: Books and Borrowers

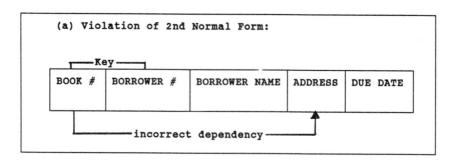

(a) Violation of 2nd Normal Form:

BOOK #	BORROWER #	BORROWER NAME	ADDRESS	DUE DATE

Key

incorrect dependency

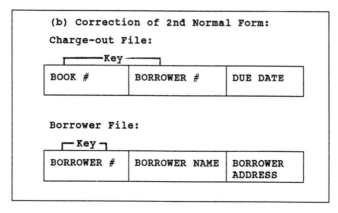

(b) Correction of 2nd Normal Form:

Charge-out File:

BOOK #	BORROWER #	DUE DATE

Key

Borrower File:

BORROWER #	BORROWER NAME	BORROWER ADDRESS

Key

Rule 3 (Third Normal Form)

This rule states that no field must be dependent on another field that is not a key. In other words, each field must be identified by the key, not another field. Figure 3.8(a) shows a violation of this rule.

The bibliographic file contains a book number (which is the key), title, publisher, and, incorrectly, the publisher's address and telephone number. It violates our sense of things to even mix publisher's addresses and telephone numbers with bibliographic data. The publisher's *name* is correctly relevant to the book number, but the address and telephone number are relevant, not to the book number, but to the publisher's name.

What does it matter? If a publisher changes its telephone number, you might have to scan through hundreds of records to find and change every occurrence of the telephone number. Also, if you discard the last book by a publisher, its name, address, and telephone number are gone. Lastly, you have no information about a particular publisher until you buy at least one book from it.

FIGURE 3.8 Third Normal Form: Publishers

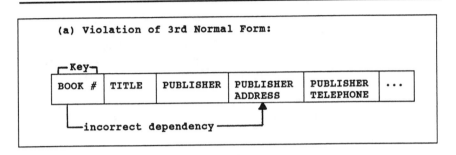

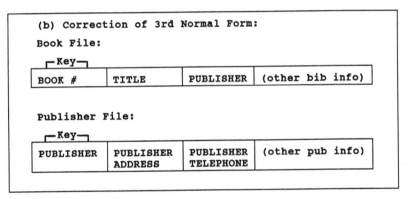

The solution? Remove the publisher's address and telephone number and put them with the publisher's name into a separate file—a publisher information file. See Figure 3.8(b). Now to update a telephone number, you need change only one record, not several hundred (of course, if the publisher changes its *name*, you have a problem). Also, you can maintain publisher's information even if you have no items in the collection from that publisher.

Notice that the publisher's name is the key in the second file. The common field of publisher's name allows the relationship to be established. There must be a common field between any two files, and it should be the key in at least one of them.

An important caveat: Brooks[3] argues that if the data (here, the address and telephone number) are important for legal or archival purposes, then it may be important to keep them in the bibliographic file. That is, it may be worth violating this rule if you need to keep a "snapshot" of the conditions that existed at the time the item was purchased. This is workable for archival files but not for active and volatile ones.

Endnotes

1. Several books are recommended for a deeper understanding of database models: Michael J. Freiling. *Understanding Database Management* (Sherman Oaks, Calif.: Alfred Publishing Co., 1982); Shaku Atre. *Database; Structured Techniques for Design, Performance, and Management.* 2d ed. (New York: Wiley, 1988); David Kroenke. *Database Processing.* 2d ed. (Chicago: Science Research Associates, 1983).
2. Database purists do not like to use the term fields, records, and files. Instead, they use attributes, tuples, and relations. Microcomputer database managers usually use the former terminology, and I will stick with it here.
3. Terrance Brooks, manuscript of book: *From Data to Database* (Englewood Cliffs, N.J.: Prentice-Hall).

Part 2

dBASE Serials System Application

4

Introduction To The Serials System

Having covered some basics about computers, files, and databases, let's turn now to a specific task: developing a serials information system using dBASE. Suppose a small library wishes to establish a system to automate its serials check-in. The library owns a microcomputer and a printer, and a staff person (rightly or wrongly called a "systems analyst") who knows something about database management programs. This person has already done a *systems analysis* to find out whether a computerized system would be worthwhile, what should be in the database, what printouts are necessary and desirable, and who will be using it. He or she has planned the details necessary in setting up a system. The serials activities of this hypothetical library have outgrown the present manual system, but are small enough to implement on a microcomputer using dBASE.

Here are the information management processes involved in setting up a system. I will discuss most of these in detail in later chapters.

Planning the Database: Fields, Records, Files
The analyst must do two things almost simultaneously: organize the data into fields, and decide how to put the fields into files so as not to violate the rules for database design. Before any data go into the computer, our hypothetical librarian/analyst must decide how the data will be broken down.

Creating Data Files and Capturing Data
Files must be created to hold data, and programs written to capture data. Some data may be on cards from an old, manual system. Some

may be on tapes or disks from another project. Most likely, the data will be *keyboarded*—typed at a computer keyboard.

Verifying and Categorizing Data

The programs may use routines for verifying whether the data are complete, fall within acceptable ranges, are alphabetical or numerical, do not conflict with other data, and so on.

Storage and Retrieval of Information

The data will be stored on disks. Disk storage and retrieval are at the heart of information management. Retrieval is usually selective. The analyst must think about methods for selectively retrieving information.

Making Data Meaningful—Classifying and Arranging

Pieces of data remain raw until classified and arranged, two very important operations. You do these usually in preparation for printing or displaying the information. Classification means putting like data together, and is probably the most important (certainly the most ubiquitous) information processing task. Arranging means to sort into a predetermined sequence, for example, alphabetically, or by date. The analyst must decide how data should be arranged. A strength of the computer is the ability to take randomly arranged data and rearrange them on demand, to meet specific needs.

Developing a Working System

The analyst must think about the whole in terms of its functional parts, and the parts in terms of how they will work together as a whole. He or she must develop user interfaces: instructions, menus, screens, and other information to present to the user.

A fully developed Serials System would consist of many programs, database files, indexes, and an assortment of other files for screen and report formatting. One or the other of the programs is always in control, working with a database management system (DBMS).

DATABASE MANAGEMENT SYSTEMS

A DBMS is a program, or set of programs, to create, update, search, report, sort, and relate files in a variety of ways to meet a variety of needs. The DBMS handles the chore of bringing data from many files, processing the data, and getting everything to the right person at the right time.

Some DBMS's require you to work within the constraints of the system itself. That is, the DBMS dictates the appearance of screens, reports, data entry methods, ways of searching, and so on. You are stuck with doing things its way. More powerful systems (like dBASE) provide, in addition, a way to write custom programs. Your programs are limited only by your imagination and abilities as a programmer. You can create fancy or plain data entry screens, complex or simple printed reports. You can search with complex search statements or simple ones, give or not give the user help along the way, and generally control what you want to have the system do.

dBASE III PLUS AND dBASE IV AS MANAGEMENT SYSTEMS

I will be using dBASE to illustrate some techniques for programming a Serials System. Because dBASE is now available in several versions, a brief excursion into its history may be helpful.

dBASE had its beginnings at the California Institute of Technology's Jet Propulsion Laboratory in 1979. Wayne Ratliff was working with mainframe data managers and developed a database manager for home computers. He named it VULCAN and advertised his creation in *Byte* magazine. He sold only 50 copies, although it was more powerful than any other microcomputer data manager of that day.

In 1980, George Tate, a software distributor, bought the rights to VULCAN. He changed the name to dBASE II. Some people woke up one morning and wondered how they had missed dBASE I, but there never was a dBASE I!

Tate engaged in a vigorous advertising campaign and sold more than 2000 copies per month. He formed Ashton-Tate, Inc. to develop and market dBASE II. It was primitive by today's standards. It lacked menus, had little on-screen help, and came with a horrid manual. But, it included a program language to write custom applications, could work with two files at once (most managers at the time could only work with one), and was esoteric enough to garner a nearly cultist following among microcomputer buffs.

dBASE II set the standard for microcomputer data managers, and turned many computer enthusiasts to CP/M, the operating system on which it ran. It also divided the database management world into camps of those who opted for ease of use (it was not easy to use) and those who sought power and flexibility at all costs (it was powerful). dBASE II and a spreadsheet program called Visicalc probably were responsible for selling more microcomputers than all computer salespersons combined.

By the 1980s, microcomputers had become much faster, more powerful, and had greater memory capacities. Old software would not work on these new computers. dBASE II and CP/M were showing their ages, so a new version, dBASE III, was introduced in 1984 to take advantage of the power of the new computers. It was more powerful, had a more extensive language, and more on-screen helps and menus. dBASE III was a new program, not a revision of dBASE II, and the two are not very compatible. Although there are some dBASE II applications in use, it is no longer available for sale, and its use in libraries is dwindling.

dBASE III Plus (+), introduced in 1985, added more enhancements, including a much better user interface and menu-driven mode. It was a revision of III and all commands in III work in III+ (but not the other way around). There are many dBASE III and III+ applications in use, and dBASE III+ is still available, as of this writing.

dBASE IV came out in 1989. It is based on III+ and is "upward" compatible with it (programs and files created in III+ work with IV, but not the other way around). It has many new and enhanced commands, functions, and capabilities. It is also much larger. dBASE III+ comes on 2 floppy disks and is useable on a dual floppy machine. dBASE IV is delivered on 14 floppies and requires a hard disk machine. In 1991, Ashton-Tate was purchased by Borland International, producers of a competitive DBMS called "Paradox."

All the illustrations in this book will work with either dBASE III+ or IV. The Serials System, sample programs, and illustrations can be "migrated" to IV with practically no changes.

dBASE FILES

Chapter 1 explained how a working system piles programs on top of programs, each interacting with each, and eventually all working through DOS and ROM to affect the hardware and get something done. Our system will be no exception. First, the dBASE program, itself, is a set of files, called the dBASE System Files. These are required for all applications, and dBASE will handle the interaction of these. We need not be concerned with them, except to make sure they are on the disk and directory that we are using.

We will create several other files as we develop the Serials System, each serving a special purpose. These are our responsibility. dBASE asks us to name any files we create. Then, depending on the kind of file, dBASE adds an extension. Extensions have special meanings. Data are stored in specialized formats each of which serves particular processing functions. The extensions indicate the format. Some of the most common ones are:

Extension	Kind of File	Description
.DBF	Database	Database file

Extension	Kind of File	Description
.PRG	Program	Command language program
.DBT	Memo	Special data field
.NDX	Index	Index to database file
.FMT	Format	Custom screen instructions
.LBL	Label	Label printing instructions
.MEM	Memory	Contents of memory
.FRM	Report	Report instructions
.CAT	Catalog	Sets of related files

It is important to know that you may give the same extension to several files with the same name. BIB.DBF, BIB.FMT, and BIB.NDX are three different files, each serving a specialized function (in this case: a database, a screen format, and an index). Usually the context in which they are used makes it clear to dBASE which one is called for.

MODES OF OPERATION

dBASE III+ and dBASEIV have three modes of operation: Assist (called the Control Center in IV), Interactive (sometimes called Dot Prompt), and Program. Assist is easiest to use, but is the least powerful. The Interactive Mode adds power but requires the user to know hundreds of commands. The Program Mode is the most powerful, but it requires much work to write programs. You use all three modes in developing programs.

The Assist Mode (or, simply, Assist) is menu driven. You do everything through a series of menus. You do not need to know dBASE commands, just how to navigate the menus. You get into this mode by typing ASSIST at the dot prompt, or you may arrange to have dBASE begin in this mode.

You cannot save dBASE III+ Assist keystrokes in a file (*data* are saved in a database but not the *processing steps*). Repetitive tasks using Assist require going though the same motions each time. dBASE IV does have a handy macro facility with which keys pressed while in the Control Center can be recorded, saved, and played back at will. This is useful for simple repetitive tasks, but is no substitute for programming.

Assist is best for beginners, especially those who have no desire or need to learn programming. Assist is a simple way to tap standard features and power of dBASE's relational management system. It is especially useful during some phases of program development, most notably file creation and input screen "painting," as we shall soon see.

dBASE IV has greatly improved its Control Center. It is powerful, flexible, and more complex. Even so, you cannot use it alone to create stand-alone information management systems.

The Interactive Mode, also called Command Mode, Immediate Mode, or Dot Prompt Mode, allows the user to type commands directly from the keyboard. These are often called "dot prompt commands" because dBASE places a dot in the lower left corner of the screen, indicating it is ready for a command. To make effective use of this mode requires knowledge of several hundred commands, what they do, and when to use them. This is the least reliable method. There is a great chance of making a mistake that will destroy valuable data. The burden rests with the user to know and use the commands.

Command mode is more flexible than Assist, but less so than the Program Mode. Once you have learned a few commands, it can be faster than Assist to use. It allows quick interaction with databases. You can quickly change files, test the contents of data fields, sum, average, and count data quickly. You can test programming routines, and try out new things.

Programming is the most flexible and powerful way to use dBASE. Commands are placed in files called programs that control the management, manipulation, and use of the databases. Even simple tasks take a fair amount of time to program, debug, set up, and get working. But, once you have a correctly running program, it will have been time well spent.

Programs may be compiled and executed as completely stand-alone without having dBASE in sight. Compilation of dBASE programs requires a separate compiler.

Programs are sometimes difficult to develop but very simple to use. Once you have written a program, the end-user does not need to know dBASE commands or even how to work the Assist menu. He or she needs only the barest information to get things started.

During program development, you can easily make mistakes that will destroy valuable data. It is best to develop programs with small amounts of sample data. Once programs are running properly there is less chance that the user will destroy data, especially if back-ups are kept. In other words, programming puts the greatest burden on the designer/developer/programmer but the least on the end-user.

All three modes have strengths and weaknesses and each is useful for certain tasks. We will use all three at different times to develop the Serials System program.

I will use several conventions when describing dBASE programs and programming:

Unless otherwise noted, the examples use dBASE III+ since it is widely used in libraries and programs are easily transported to IV. If IV provides significant enhancements or changes, I will describe them. Significant differences are signaled by : **IV**

The first mention of a particular data file will use its full name (e.g., BIB.DBF) while later close-by references will usually omit the extension (e.g., BIB).

I will use upper-case letters for dBASE commands, file names, variable names, and program examples. You should know, however, that dBASE makes no distinction between upper and lower case, except for words within quotation marks.

Most commands used as illustration may be issued either at the dot prompt or in programs. The dot has been omitted since it is not used in programs, and, in fact, is never typed. A few commands cannot be used at the dot prompt and these will be so identified.

Some command descriptions use <expn> or (expn). This is an abbreviation of *expression*. This means that variables, constants, fields, database names, arithmetic calculations, and functions can be substituted for expn, depending on the command. If expn is enclosed in brackets, <expn>, the expression should be typed without parenthesis; if enclosed in parenthesis (expn), they should be used.

Some of my command descriptions have words in brackets or parenthesis, for example <database name> or (variable). This gives more detail about the kind of data that should be substituted.

dBASE commands and program statements are often too long to fit on one line. Command lines and statements that end in a semicolon mean that the next line is a continuation of the command. The following example is one command. The semicolon also may be used in this way in programs:

```
JOIN WITH BIB TO CLAIMS FOR ISSN = BIB->ISSN;
AND ACTION = "F" FIELDS BIB->TITLE, BIB->AGENT_CODE;
    COPY, YR, MON
```

Lines within programs or program illustrations beginning with an asterisk (*) are comments, as are words within lines preceded by a double ampersand (&&). These are not part of commands, and are ignored by the interpreter. This is standard dBASE use:

```
*THIS IS A COMMENT
DISPLAY FOR COST = 0 && This IS A COMMENT ADDED TO A
COMMAND
```

Most of the sample programs have numbered lines. *dBASE does not use or allow numbered lines.* I have included them here only for textual analysis. Do not include line numbers in dBASE programs.

5

Creating dBASE Files

We begin the Serials System by creating several database files. Technically, databases are collections of data files. However, dBASE gives the name "database" to single data files. I will refer to dBASE databases as files or database files. File creation is a two step process:

1. Creation of a file structure
This activity places an "empty container" on the disk that will eventually hold data. It contains defined structural information so that data will "fit" when it is later added. Careful thought should be given to this step because, more than almost anything else, it will enhance or limit later information management.

This step must be done outside the programming environment. Although programs can create new files from already existing ones, you must begin the process in the Assist or Interactive Modes.

dBASE allows you to add, delete, and rename fields after putting data in them. Even so, I recommend that the database be properly designed from the beginning.

2. Adding data to the structure
This step involves putting actual data (records) into the file. It may be done by the designer but is usually a continuing operation during the life of the system. This chapter discusses file structures, and chapter 8 will show how to add data.

dBASE FILE ORGANIZATION

Before creating the files, we should know something about how dBASE organizes them.

Fixed Length, Random Organization

dBASE uses a random file organization with fixed-length records. Each record contains the same named fields, in the same order. Each record is the same total length.

The fixed-length field structure is a major weakness of dBASE. Some data, like textual materials, do not lend themselves to fixed-length records, and are less appropriate for dBASE. Others, like the serials data, are more appropriate. Even here, you may have a problem in deciding how long to make each field. For example, 30 characters assigned to the title field will be too short for some titles and too long for some. You must decide whether to truncate long titles or waste space on short ones. Care must be given to the task of assigning appropriate field lengths (dBASE calls them field widths).

dBASE maintains the field names, field types, and widths as part of the file. A "header" holds this information and precedes the first record. It is generally invisible to the user.

Because field names are stored with the data, programmers must use the same names in all later references. Languages like COBOL and BASIC allow programming reassignment of field names, but dBASE does not. Every program that refers to a file must use the assigned field names.

Dynamic Record Numbers

Each new record is assigned a relative record number (RRN). However, the RRNs in dBASE differ from other random files in the following ways:

1. They bear no relationship to the file data. There is no inherent relationship between the data in a record and its physical location in the file.
2. They change as records are added and deleted. dBASE normally adds new records with new RRNs to the end of the file. When you delete records, all higher numbered ones move up and are given new RRNs. Although you can use record numbers for retrieval, keeping track of them is usually not worth the effort.

Current Record and Record Pointer

An important thing to know about is the *current record*. The current record is the default record that will have action done to it, unless you specify otherwise. When you open (reference) a file, the current record is the first record in the database, or if indexed, the first in the index.

dBASE automatically keeps track of the current record in a variable called the *record pointer*. Some commands only move the record pointer without taking other action. Other commands change, delete, or display current record data. Still other commands change, delete, or display data from the current record forward for a specified number of records. You can determine the current record number by issuing the following command (either from the dot prompt or in a program): ? RECNO() .

SERIALS SYSTEM FILE STRUCTURES

The Serials System uses several database files. We have already seen why it is not wise to include all data in one file. To set the stage for the discussion to follow, I will describe the major database files.

BIB.DBF: This is the main file. It contains bibliographic data about serials that are stable for all copies: ISSN, title, publisher, frequency, and so on. This file will contain one record for each title that the library owns. Figure 5.1 shows the structure (the column marked "Comments" is not in dBASE; I added it here by way of explanation). BIB.DBF only contains data about the serial as a bibliographic entity. It does not contain data about individual copies (to do so would violate Rule #1 in chapter 3), nor does it include check-in data (to do so would violate Rule #2). It includes the name of the publisher but in order not to violate Rule #3, a separate file holds the remaining publisher data (address, telephone number, etc.).

FIGURE 5.1   BIB.DBF Structure

```
Structure for database: BIB.DBF

Field   Field Name   Type        Width   Dec   Comments

   1    ISSN         Character      9

   2    TITLE        Character     30

   3    FREQ         Character      2           Frequency

   4    PUBLISHER    Character     30

   5    NOS_VOL      Numeric        2      0    Numbers/vol

   6    VOL_YR       Numeric        2      0    Vols/year
**  Total  **                     76
```

COPY.DBF: This file holds data specific to specific copies, such as cost, subscription due date, and vendor. There is one record for each copy owned by the library. Copy data are more changeable than bibliographic data as two copies of the same title may have very different subscription due dates, costs, vendors, and so on. The structure is shown in Figure 5.2. The common ISSN field ties COPY and BIB together. I have omitted accounting information (such as P.O., invoice, and account numbers) from this file for simplicity. It could include accounting data, or they might be stored in a separate file, or even in a separate system.

FIGURE 5.2   COPY.DBF Structure

```
Structure for database: COPY.DBF

Field   Field Name   Type         Width    Dec    Comments

   1    ISSN         Character      9

   2    COPY         Numeric        2        0     Copy number

   3    VEND_CODE    Character      2              Vendor

   4    COST         Numeric        7        2

   5    SUB_DATE     Date           8              Sub due date

   6    FIRST_DATE   Date           8              1st rcvd date

   7    FIRST_VOL    Numeric        4              1st rcvd vol

   8    NOTES        Memo          10

** Total **                        51
```

MREC.DBF; WREC.DBF; DREC.DBF: These three files hold the check-in records for monthly (including bimonthly, annual, irregular), weekly (and biweekly), and daily serials. Most of the data in these files concern the date, volume, and issue for each item checked in. There will be one record for each checked-in issue of each copy. Figure 5.3 shows the structure of MREC.DBF. The only bibliographic information in these files are ISSN and COPY, which serve to link the check-in files with COPY.DBF. The two other files are identical except that WREC and DREC have additional fields to hold the week of the month and day of the month, respectively.

FIGURE 5.3   MREC.DBF Structure

```
Structure for database: MREC.DBF

Field   Field Name   Type        Width     Dec     Comments

   1    ISSN         Character      9

   2    COPY         Numeric        2        0

   3    YR           Character      4                Issue year

   4    MON          Character      2                Issue month

   5    ACTION       Character      1                Action code

   6    VOL          Numeric        4        0       Issue vol no

   7    ISSUE        Numeric        4        0       Issue no

   8    TOD          Date           8                Today's date

** Total **                        35
```

PUB.DBF: This is a file of publisher's names and addresses. Its structure is shown in Figure 5.4. The PUBLISHER field ties PUB and BIB together.

CREATING THE STRUCTURE OF BIB.DBF

The best way to create a new file is through the Assist mode. The main component is a menu bar at the top of the screen. Also important is a message line at the very bottom of the screen. This line gives instructions of what to do next. Pay particular attention to this line.

Use the right/left arrow keys to choose menu options from the top menu bar. This highlights each choice. When the desired choice is lit, press **Return** (or, depending on the computer model, **Enter**).

Choosing a main option usually causes "pull-down" submenus appropriate to the main choice to appear. Use the up/down arrow keys to highlight these choices, and press **Return**. Choosing a submenu option may open other submenu choices. Choose these with the up/down arrow keys. To "back out" of a submenu, use **Esc** to return to the next higher level submenu.

FIGURE 5.4   PUB.DBF Structure

```
Structure for database: B:pub.dbf

Field   Field Name   Type        Width     Dec

    1   PUBLISHER    Character      30

    2   ADDR         Character      30

    3   SUITE        Character      30

    4   CITY         Character      30

    5   STATE        Character       2

    6   ZIP          Numeric         5        0

    7   COUNTRY      Character      20

    8   PARENT_CO    Character      30

    9   TELEPHONE    Character      14
```

It is impossible to show the constantly changing Assist screen on paper. I will use the following conventions to describe Assist menu options:

1. All Assist options are shown in bold type.
2. Only the options that are then needed are shown, not the array of possibilities.
3. Menu and submenu options are shown with slashes (/) between them. For example, **Create/database file/B:BIB** means to choose or type each of these in turn, as new options are displayed.
4. Some operations require passing through the menu more than once. This will be shown by a new line of choices under a previous set:
   Create/Format for Screen/B:BIB.
   Update/Append

Naming the Database File

dBASE III asks you to name the database file before creating it, while dBASE IV asks for a name after creating the structure. In either case, the name may be up to eight characters, the first of which must be a letter. The others can be letters, numeric digits, or the underscore (_), but no other punctuation marks or spaces. dBASE automatically assigns an extension of .DBF. Choose a name that is meaningful.

Now, to create BIB.DBF. Choose the following options by using the arrow keys to highlight the choice and pressing **Return** to choose it:

dBASE III+ Assist Mode:
Create/Database file/C: this is the drive that contains the disk holding the files.
Enter the name of the file: BIB

dBASE IV Control Center:
Data/create (in addition, dBASE IV asks whether you wish to **index on each field**—choose N for now. Before leaving the Control Center, **Name the file**—use BIB).

Describing Fields

The next screen asks for the name of each field, its type, width, and number of decimal places. Type the information asked for and press **Return** (or **Enter**, ↵) each time. Refer to Figure 5.1 for the structure. When you have finished describing all fields, press **Ctrl** and **End** simultaneously. See Figure 5.5.

Field Names
Type in the name (e.g., TITLE) and hit **Return**. This, of course, is the permanent name of the field, not the data that the field will hold. You should choose names that are descriptive instead of cryptic (e.g., TITLE instead of T), but they must follow these rules:

- Field names can be no more than ten characters long.
- They must begin with a letter.
- They cannot contain blank spaces.
- Only letters, numbers, and the underscore may be used.

Field Types
Type the first letter of one of the following kinds and hit **Return**. dBASE III uses five field types, and IV has six:

FIGURE 5.5   File Creation Screen

```
                                                    Bytes remaining:   3925

              Field Name   Type        Width  Dec        Field Name   Type   Width  Dec

          1   ISSN         Character      9
          2   TITLE        Character     30
          3   FREQ         Character      2
          4   PUBLISHER    Character     30
          5   NOS_VOL      Numeric        2    0
          6   VOL_YR       Numeric        2    0



CREATE        ||<C:>||BIB                              ||Field: 6/6         ║        ║
                              Enter the field name.
Field names begin with a letter and may contain letters, digits and underscores
```

- *Character.* Character fields may contain any character on the keyboard. The maximum size is 254 characters in any one field. You can put numbers in character fields if you do not plan to do arithmetic with them.
- *Numeric.* These may contain only numbers, the decimal point, and negative sign. Use numeric fields to store arithmetic data. They may be up to 19 digits long, including a decimal point and negative sign, but only the first 15 digits are significant. Even if you do not anticipate doing math or arithmetic comparisons with numeric data, it is usually best to store them as *Numeric*. The reason for this is that numbers sort differently from characters. For example, ages stored as *Character* type will sort like this: 1, 10, 11, 19, 2, 20, whereas if stored as *Numeric* type, they will sort more normally: 1, 2, 10, 11, 19, 20.

   IV   dBASE IV has an additional numeric type called *Float* that stores floating point numbers a bit more efficiently than usual numeric storage.
- *Date.* Date fields hold only valid calendar dates. They are usually entered and displayed as mm/dd/yy, although on the file they are actually stored as yyyymmdd. Date fields are always eight bytes long. Dates can be stored as *Character* type, but usually they should be stored as *Date* type. The decision depends on whether you anticipate using date functions or string functions on them (see chapter 8). The single year (e.g., 1990) may be stored as *Character* or *Numeric* type, depending on what you plan to do with it.
- *Logical.* Logical fields are always only one character. They may contain only the letters Y, y, N, n, T, t, F, f, corresponding to Yes, No, True, False.

   Logical data are of a binary, yes/no, true/false nature. They can be a powerful information processing ally. Beiser uses them in a serials control system to store yes/no answers to a series of questions—e.g., GIFT? BIND? MICROFORM? MONTHLY? WEEKLY? DAILY?[1]
- *Memo.* Memo fields store large blocks of free-form information, up to 5000 characters. A memo field only takes up ten bytes in the main file. The actual textual information is stored in a second file. Memo fields are very poorly integrated in dBASE III.

   IV Memo fields have been greatly improved in dBASE IV. The size of a memo field is virtually unlimited. More important, there are new commands to retrieve selective data from memo fields, correcting a serious weakness in III.[2]

Widths

Next, you must specify the width of character and numeric fields in terms of the number of characters or digits. Remember, dBASE uses fixed-length fields (except for memo fields), so you must choose field lengths that are long enough to hold typical data, but not so long as to waste space. If you choose a width of, say, 50 for the title, *every* record in the database will have 50 characters dedicated to the title.

Decimals

For numeric fields, you additionally supply the number of decimal places (DEC). The width of numeric fields must be large enough to include the decimal point, the decimal digits, and the sign (if there is one). For example, a serial cost of $125.54 would require a width of six with two decimals (the "$" is not stored).

You create each database the same way: (1) name the database, (2) name each field, (3) determine the type of each field, and (4) determine the size of each field. You may optionally add data now, but I will hold off describing this step until a later chapter.

It is a good idea to keep a notebook of the names and structures of your files. It is frustrating to be in the middle of writing a program and not remember the name you gave to a field. dBASE can help here. Obtain a printout of the structure of each database by issuing the following commands at the dot prompt:

```
USE BIB (or COPY, MREC, etc.)
DISPLAY STRUCTURE TO PRINT
```

CHANGING A DATABASE STRUCTURE

dBASE allows you to change the structure of an existing database, even after it has records in it. You may do this either through Assist or the dot prompt:

```
    dBASE III+ Assist Mode:
Setup/Database file/C:BIB.DBF
Modify/Database file
```

```
    dBASE IV Control Center:
Data/BIB/Modify structure
```

```
    From the dot prompt, type:
USE BIB
MODIFY STRUCTURE.
```

You will be taken back to the database creation screen and may add fields or change characteristics of existing fields. Use the arrow keys to move the cursor to any field on the screen. To insert a new field between two, press **Ctrl N**. To delete a field, press **Ctrl U**. Hit **Ctrl End** to quit.

A couple of words of caution are in order, especially if the database already contains data. As you might expect, if you add a field, it will be empty in already existing records. If you delete a field, you delete all data already in that field from all records. Do not change the name of a field and also its length or type in the same MODIFY STRUCTURE session. You will lose data if you do. If you must change both the name and anything else, do it in two sessions. It is not advisable to change a field from numeric to character if the field already contains data.

We have used Assist to create the structure of the Serial System files. They are empty structures at this point with no actual data. We will create input screens in chapter 9 to put data into the databases, but first, an excursion into the fundamentals of dBASE programming.

Endnotes

1. Karl Beiser. *Essential Guide to dBASE III in Libraries* (Westport, Conn.: Meckler, 1987).
2. Neil Yerkey, "Enhanced Memo Field Processing," *Computers in Libraries* Febuary, 1990, 10 (2): 35-36.

6

dBASE Programming

Chapter 5 explained how to use Assist for initial creation of file structures. Most of the rest of the Serials System requires programming, and
this chapter begins the exploration of how to write programs in dBASE's
command language. Programming is part science, part art, and, it
seems, part smoke and mirrors. It can be so frustrating when things go
wrong and so exhilarating when they come together. Some people take
to it like ducks to water, others never get the hang of it and swear off
programming, and sometimes computers, forever.

WHY PROGRAM?

You can do much with the Assist and Control Center modes of
dBASE. They are powerful, flexible, and versatile—taking care of many
of your data management needs without programming. Why program,
then? Programming gives these advantages:

- Although you can do much through Assist/Control Center, you
  cannot do everything. Many of the routines and tricks described
  in the following chapters just cannot be done without programming. Programming is the best way to develop unique, customized, or complex applications.
- Assist/Control Center requires the *user* to know dBASE; programming requires only that the *designer* know it. If the designer and
  the user are the same person, this advantage is minimized. Often,
  customized programs are turned over to persons who neither
  know, nor care to learn, dBASE. They just want a workable sys-

tem, and programs are best for stand-alone, user-friendly applications.

- Repetitious operations in Assist/Control Center can be tiresome since it keeps no record of processing steps. Programs are best for repetitious, often used operations.
- Programming helps to develop self-discipline, logical thinking, and attention to detail. It also robs one of sleep, friends, and sunshine. You can become obsessed with it. Like playing chess with a formidable opponent, it tends to dominate your thoughts. But, it can be fun.
- One thing is certain: it is the only way to get the most from dBASE III or IV. The Assist and Interactive Modes have their uses, but programming best exploits the power of a relational database.

This chapter will introduce some important ideas related to programming, and the next chapter will examine some useful functions and commands in detail. Later, I will expand on these ideas as we continue to develop the Serials System.

dBASE programs are files of dBASE commands. A single command issued at the dot prompt, will cause one thing to happen immediately. A file of commands, taken together, constitutes a program. Such files are called *command files* or, more often, *programs*.

The terminology is a bit confusing. Technically, statements typed at the dot prompt are *commands* while those same statements used in programs are *instructions*. But, because dBASE uses the same language for both modes, programmers usually refer to them all as commands. I will follow this practice and call them commands whether used at the dot prompt or in programs. When I refer to various words and instructions that are not commands (flow structures, functions, parts of commands), I will call them *statements*.

There are more than 150 commands and statements in dBASE III+, and more than 350 in dBASE IV. Most dot prompt commands can be used in programs; a few cannot be, a few should not be, and there are a few program-only statements.

WRITING PROGRAMS

Using the Built-in Editor

dBASE has a built-in editor for writing programs. It is adequate for short programs, although it has limited flexibility. To use the editor, type the following at the dot prompt:

```
MODIFY COMMAND <program name>
```

This may be abbreviated to MODI COMM. The <program name> may be any legitimate DOS name of eight or fewer characters. dBASE automatically adds .PRG to it. It is a good idea to use names that are as meaningful as possible within the eight-character restraint.

For example, type the following to create the main menu program of our Serials System:

```
MODIFY COMMAND MAINMENU
```

You will then be given a blank screen on which to type program statements, one per line, ending each with a carriage return. The maximum length of a command in dBASE III+ is 254 characters (including spaces), and 1024 characters in dBASE IV. Most are fewer than 80 characters. If a command is longer than 80 characters, just keep typing—the editor wraps to the next line. Sometimes, however, you may deliberately want to break a long command into several lines. To do so, end each line with a ";" and a carriage return, as shown here (don't worry now about what this command does):

```
JOIN WITH BIB TO CLAIMS FOR ISSN = BIB->ISSN;
AND ACTION = 'F' FIELDS BIB->TITLE, BIB->AGENT_CODE;
COPY, YR, MON
```

You can also use the editor to change existing programs. If the program already exists, the editor automatically calls it in for editing.

You cannot enter the editor from Assist in dBASE III+. You must type MODIFY COMMAND from the dot prompt. dBASE IV has a Control Center choice called **Create Program.**

dBASE is not particular about how you use upper and lower case, blank spaces, blank lines, and indentations in program statements, *unless they are within quoted strings.* In the following examples, (a) and (b) are equivalent in 1. and 2. but not in 3.:

```
1.   (a) LINECOUNT = LINECOUNT + 2
     (b) linecount = linecount+2


2. (a) IF EOF()
           CLOSE DATABASES
           QUIT
       ENDIF
   (b) if eof()
         close databases
         quit
         endif
```

3.   (a) LOCATE FOR TITLE = "BYTE"
     (b) LOCATE FOR TITLE = "Byte"

Use spaces, blank lines, upper/lower case, and indentations to make the program more readable. You may use either single quotes (') or double quotes (") with strings, providing you use the same kind at both ends (e.g., LOCATE FOR TITLE = 'Byte' is acceptable).

dBASE's editor is a full-screen editor, meaning you can use the arrow keys, **PgUp,** and **PgDn** to move the cursor around the screen. You can type anywhere on the screen or use **BackSpace** or **Del** to delete characters and the **Insert** to insert characters and lines.

When you wish to quit editing and save the results, press **Ctrl W**. To exit the editor without saving the results, press **Ctrl Q** or **Esc**. Other editing keys are shown in the manual, as well as on the editing screen, itself.

Problems With the dBASE III Editor

The dBASE III+ editor has several weaknesses. One is that you cannot do block moves. To move or copy sections of your program to another location within the program, you must retype them. Also, you cannot delete an entire block, but only a line at a time. Nor is there a search feature to locate words or phrases.

Worse, the maximum program length the editor can handle is 4096 characters. This is about 120 lines. The editor just chops off any programs that are longer. If the words "Program too long . . ." appear at the top of the screen, do NOT save the file. Exit without saving **(Esc)**. The advice in the next paragraph may help.

Using a Word Processor

A solution to III's editor problems is to use a separate text editor or word processor so long as it will save text as pure ASCII files. Most word processors can save ASCII files. You can even integrate your favorite word processor into dBASE as the editor. An excellent program editor for this purpose is WordPerfect Program Editor, which is part of the WordPerfect Library (WordPerfect Corporation, Orem, Utah). It has powerful word processing capabilities and automatically saves programs in ASCII.

The best solution is to put your word processor or program editor into the same directory as dBASE and invoke it by typing RUN PE (or WS, or whatever your word processor is called) or:

    ! PE

When you exit the word processor, you go back to dBASE automatically.

IV The built-in editor has been much improved in dBASE IV. It has block copy and move capabilities, automatic indentation, and a menu interface. It can edit programs of up to 32,000 lines, compared to 120 lines in dBASE III+.

dBASE COMMAND STRUCTURE

We will now look at the general makeup of dBASE commands, including how to use a few important ones. The next chapter will explain particular commands and command options more systematically.

Command Verbs

Each program command begins on a new line. The first word of a command is usually a command verb, followed by various expressions, scope statements, and conditions that affect the operation of the command. The verb tells the computer what to do. Here are a few examples of verbs:

> CLEAR   Clears the screen.
> READ   Permits entry of data from the keyboard.
> APPEND Adds records to the file.
> LIST   Lists the contents of a file.

One command uses no verb. It is the assignment statement (=). The verb STORE is implied and can be used instead. Statements (a) and (b) in each of these examples are equivalent:

```
1.   (a) A = B
     (b) STORE B TO A
2.   (a) AGE = 30
     (b) STORE 30 TO AGE
```

One verb should be explained right away because I must use it now and throughout the rest of this book. It is the question mark (?). Programmers have long used this symbol to mean "show or display" (BASIC programmers will recognize it). In all the examples that follow it means "display what follows on the screen."

Most verbs may be abbreviated to the first four letters *of each word* in it. For example, DISPLAY may be shortened to DISP, DELETE to DELE, REINDEX to REIN, DISPLAY STRUCTURE to DISP STRU, MODIFY COMMAND to MODI COMM, and so on.

Expressions

Some verbs are used alone. Others may be followed by expressions, scope statements, or conditions which help define and shape the action required. Expressions are literals (constants), operators, functions, memory variables, database file names, and field names that provide material for the verb to work on. Following are a few verbs with expressions:

? "Hello"	Displays "Hello" on the screen.
USE BIB	Opens the file called BIB.DBF.
@ 5,1 SAY TITLE	Displays the contents of the title field at row, 5 column 1 of the screen.
STORE 5 + 6 TO B	Adds 5 to 6 and stores the results in memory variable B.

Scope Statements

Some commands may contain an optional scope statement that indicates the number of database file records affected by the command. For example:

DISPLAY	Displays the current record only.
DISPLAY NEXT 5	Displays the next 5 records, from the current record.
DISPLAY REST	Displays the rest of the records (from the current record to the end of the file).

Conditions

Many commands compare one value with another as a basis for taking a course of action. The general form of a conditional comparison is:

```
verb FOR/WHILE <value> <operator> <value>
```

FOR/WHILE are optional parameters used by some commands. FOR means to do whatever the verb asks to all records that meet the condition. WHILE means to execute the verb until it hits the first record that does not meet the condition.

The <value> <operator> <value> part is the condition. The values on either side of the operator may be memory variables, file fields, arithmetic expressions, functions, numbers, or strings of characters.

The operator may be one of the following symbols:

=	Equal To
<=	Less Than or Equal To
<	Less Than
>	Greater Than
>=	Greater Than or Equal To
<>	Not Equal To
#	Not Equal To

A few dBASE verbs that use conditions are:

```
AVERAGE FOR/WHILE <condition>
COUNT FOR/WHILE <condition>
DELETE FOR/WHILE <condition>
DISPLAY FOR/WHILE <condition>
CASE <condition>
DO WHILE <condition>
IF <condition>
JOIN
LOCATE FOR <condition>
REPLACE FOR/WHILE <condition>
```

Many verbs do not take conditions. Some require the use of conditions (e.g., DO WHILE, IF, CASE, LOCATE). Others may be used with or without conditions (e.g., DELETE, DISPLAY, AVERAGE, COUNT). For example:

DELETE	Deletes only the current record.
DELETE FOR COST = 0	Deletes all records that have 0 in the cost field.
COUNT	Counts the number of records in the database.
COUNT FOR FREQ = 'M'	Counts the number of records that have M in the FREQ field.

I will use the DISPLAY command to illustrate a few conditional comparisons. DISPLAY by itself places data from the current record on the screen. A condition causes it to search through the file and display data from records that match the condition. The principles illustrated here apply to other commands that use conditions:

DISPLAY FOR ISSN = MISSN	Displays all records in which ISSN equals the value stored in variable MISSN.

`DISPLAY WHILE VEND_CODE =` `"D"`	Displays records in which the vendor code is "D" until the vendor code changes.
`DISPLAY FOR COST > 100`	Displays all serials that have a number greater than 100 in the COST field.
`DISPLAY FOR COST * .08 <=` `10`	Displays all records in which 8% of the number in the COST field is equal to or less than 10.

Comparisons are evaluated as being true or false. In the above examples, a record with a true condition will be displayed; those with false conditions will be ignored.

You may negate conditions by placing .NOT. in front of the first value (the periods on either side are required). The first of the following statements finds records in which the value of the COST field is not greater than 200; the next three are equivalent and find records in which VEND_CODE does not equal D:

```
LOCATE FOR .NOT. COST > 200
LOCATE FOR .NOT. VEND_CODE = "D"
LOCATE FOR VEND_CODE <> "D"
LOCATE FOR VEND_CODE # "D".
```

Numbers must be compared with numbers (or variables and fields containing numbers), and characters with characters. You cannot mix them. Numbers are compared as expected: 1 is less than 2, which is less than 100, which is greater than 99.5, and so on. Character comparisons differ from numeric comparisons. The comparison, "JOHN" > "MARY", has nothing to do with size, age, moral virtue, or success. Comparisons of greater/lesser are based on the ASCII values of the characters making up the string.

The program compares the ASCII values of the two strings until it finds the first difference between them. In the case of "JOHN" > "MARY", the ASCII value of J is 74 and M is 77 so the statement is false since J is not greater than M. The comparison stops at that point.

The comparison: "ANDERSEN" < "ANDERSON" is true. The comparison begins with the first letter of each name and proceeds to the right until it compares the E with O. The E is less than O (alphabetically) so the comparison stops and the command does whatever it is supposed to do when conditions are true.

Upper and lower case letters make a difference here. "AMERICAN LIBRARIES" = "American Libraries" is false because "M" does not equal "m".

In its default (normal) condition, dBASE makes string comparisons letter by letter but only until it has compared all the characters on the left side of the operator. If the data on the right side of the comparison has more characters than those on the left, it does not compare the remaining characters on the right.

"JOHN" = "JOHNSON" evaluates to true. dBASE compares the word JOHN with the first 4 characters of JOHNSON; it compares letter for letter until it has no more letters on the left to compare.

The statement:

```
LOCATE FOR PUBLISHER = 'Prent'
```

would find a record in which Prentice-Hall is the publisher.

However, the comparison: "JOHNSON" = "JOHN" is false since the first seven characters on the left do not match the first seven characters on the right (of course, there are not seven characters on the right, but that in itself makes it false).

This feature can be a blessing or a curse. It can be used to find records in the file when you have only the first few characters or a few words. For example:

```
DISPLAY FOR TITLE = "America"
```

displays all records in which the title begins with the letters "America . . . ."

You can defeat this feature with the command: SET EXACT ON. Then "JOHN" would not equal "JOHNSON", "Prent" would not equal "Prentice-Hall", and "America" would not equal "American Libraries."

FULL SCREEN COMMANDS

There are a few commands that work well from the dot prompt but should be used with caution, if at all, in programs. They are called "full-screen commands." They are:

```
CREATE
BROWSE
EDIT
```

CREATE is used to create a new database file. It brings up the screen to name and size fields. It is seldom, if ever, included in programs.

BROWSE displays 23 records, one per line down the screen, with the fields going from left to right. EDIT displays only one record per screen with the fields going from top to bottom. Both allow you to view, add, change, and delete data and whole records. They are suitable for use in the Assist mode but dangerous in programs because they suspend program execution to allow the user to work with file records directly. The cursor may be moved around at will. Instructions are given at the top of the screen, and the user may merrily change data until satisfied with it.

This sounds good, but there is a problem and a danger. The problem is that the user must know what to do and how to quit doing it. My philosophy of programming is that the programmer, not the user, should be the expert in the operation of the system. The full-screen commands place too much of a burden on the wrong person.

The danger is that once you give up program control, the user may make a mistake and never get back. He or she might lose data, destroy a disk, cause the system to "freeze," or be unable to return to the program. Again, it is my belief that programs should be as fool-proof as possible. If you give up program control for the advantages of full-screen adding and editing, you invite potentially catastrophic operator error.

IV BROWSE and EDIT have been improved in dBASE IV, making them more suitable for use in programs. Options have been added that give the programmer some control over what the end-user can and cannot do. The following examples bring up the browse or edit screen to allow the user to look at records but *not* delete, change, or add to them:

```
BROWSE NODELETE NOEDIT NOAPPEND
EDIT NODELETE NOEDIT NOAPPEND
```

Use of all three options is the most restrictive. The programmer can decide how much freedom to give the end-user by omitting one or more of the above options (remember, though, the more freedom given in the full-screen commands, the more likelihood of error).

PROGRAMMING STRUCTURES

There are five "structures" used in programming. These refer to the directional sequence or flow taken by a program while it is running. They are

- Sequential
- Conditional branches
- Iterative (loop)
- Procedural branches
- Unconditional branches

Sequential Program Flow

The usual direction of program execution is from top to bottom. Commands are interpreted and executed one after the other from the top down unless the program encounters one of the other structures. Immediately after hitting and obeying a branch or loop, the program resumes its top-to-bottom flow. The following trivial program is entirely sequential, execution takes places from top to bottom:

```
USE BIB
SET PRINT ON
? "The first record in the database is:"
DISPLAY
? "The last record is:"
GO BOTTOM
DISPLAY
SET PRINT OFF
CLOSE DATABASES
QUIT
```

Conditional Branching Flow

Conditional branches cause execution of sets of different statements depending on whether a tested condition is true or false. Conditional structures are:

```
IF...ENDIF
```

IF statements test to see if some condition is true. If so, the program executes a set of statements between the IF and ENDIF. They are ignored if the condition is not true. The syntax is:

```
IF <condition>
<statements>
ENDIF
```

The following program fragment tests to see if the COST field contains a 0. If it does, it displays the quoted message on the screen. If it does not, the quoted message is ignored:

```
IF COST = 0
? "This serial is free"
ENDIF
```

If the condition is true, *all* commands between the IF and the ENDIF are executed. If false, *none* of them are executed and the program jumps to the next command after the ENDIF. Any number of dBASE commands may be between the IF and ENDIF, including other IF...ENDIFs.

Nested IF Statements
IF statements within IF statements are called *nested IFs*. The usual construction is:

```
IF <condition>
<statements>
IF <condition>
<statements>
ENDIF
<statements>
ENDIF
```

There is no limit to the nesting depth but there must be an ENDIF for every IF. Indentations are optional but are highly recommended to help the programmer keep track of the nesting.

The following fragment tests to see if the serial costs more than $100. If so, it displays the cost. If the vendor code *is also* G, it displays that it is a gift:

```
IF COST > 100
  ? "This serial costs: "
  ?? COST
  IF VEND_CODE = "G"
  ? "It is a gift."
  ENDIF
ENDIF
```

The inside set of IF statements is executed only if *both* conditions are true. If the serial is more than $100 but the vendor code is not "G," it prints the cost but skips the part about it being a gift. If the cost is $100 or less, the program skips the whole thing *even if the vendor code is "G."*

IF...ELSE...ENDIF
Another form uses an ELSE clause. This works like IF...ENDIF except the commands before the ELSE are executed if the condition is true and the commands following ELSE are executed if the condition is false. One or the other will always be executed. The usual structure is:

```
IF <condition>
<statements>
```

```
ELSE
<statements>
ENDIF
```

This example will display *either* that the serial is free or how much it costs, depending on whether or not the COST field is 0:

```
IF COST = 0
  ? "This serial is  free."
ELSE
  ? "This serial costs: "
  ?? COST
ENDIF
```

DO CASE...ENDCASE

This is a powerful conditional branching structure that makes decisions among one of several conditions. It finds the first condition that is true and takes action based on commands listed under the case. The general form is:

```
DO CASE
   CASE <condition 1>
   <execute these commands if condition 1 is true>
   CASE <condition 2>
   <execute these if condition 1 is false and 2 is true>
   CASE <conditions 3>
   <execute these if conditions 1 and 2 are false and 3 is
true>.
   OTHERWISE  [optional]
   <execute these if none of above are true>
ENDCASE
```

The following simple example illustrates this structure. The first line asks the user to type a letter on the keyboard. The letter typed is stored in the memory variable CHOICE. The DO CASE statement displays the chosen letter on the screen.

```
ACCEPT "Enter a letter from A through C" TO CHOICE
DO CASE
   CASE CHOICE = "A"
    ? "You chose the letter A."
   CASE CHOICE = "B"
    ? "You chose the letter B."
   CASE CHOICE = "C"
```

```
    ? "You chose the letter C."
  OTHERWISE
    ? "You did not choose A, B, or C as requested."
ENDCASE
```

The commands under the CASEs may be any dBASE commands, including another DO CASE. The optional OTHERWISE provides for execution of commands if none of the conditions are true. It is analogous to ELSE.

After it executes the commands under one CASE, the program skips all the rest and jumps to the statement immediately after ENDCASE. It never executes more than one case statement. The first true condition will have its commands executed. All others are ignored, *even if they are also true.*

In the following example, if the COST field in the current record is 0, the program displays that it is free. It will *not* also display that it is cheap. If COST is 5, it displays that it is cheap, but will not also display that it is moderately expensive. Only if the COST field contains a number between 10 and 99 will the program display that it is moderately expensive. If the serial costs $100 or more, nothing is displayed and the program moves on:

```
DO CASE
  CASE COST = 0
    ? "This serial is free."
  CASE COST < 10
    ? "This serial is cheap."
  CASE COST < 100
    ? "This serial is moderately expensive."
ENDCASE
```

This requires some care in devising DO CASE statements. Notice what happens if the above cases are mistakenly turned around with COST < 100 first:

```
DO CASE
  CASE COST < 100
    ? "This serial is moderately expensive."
  CASE COST < 10
    ? "This serial is cheap."
  CASE COST = 0
    ? "This serial is free."
ENDCASE
```

Here, *all* serials less than $100 would be declared as moderately expensive. The last two statements would never be displayed.

Iterative Flow

Iterative flow are commonly called loops. They execute a series of commands repeatedly while a specified condition is true.

DO WHILE...ENDDO
The syntax of dBASE's looping structure is:

```
DO WHILE <condition>
   <statements>
ENDDO
```

The commands between DO WHILE and ENDDO are executed repeatedly so long as the condition listed immediately after the DO WHILE is true. If the condition is false to start, all commands are ignored. If the condition becomes false somewhere within the loop (that is, a situation within the loop changes the condition), execution continues through the rest of the loop and on past. The only exceptions to this are if it hits the words LOOP, EXIT, DO, or RETURN. These cause the program to leave the loop immediately. They will be described later.

The following program fragment does not do much but it illustrates DO WHILE. At the beginning, X is equal to 0 so the DO WHILE condition (X < 100) is true. The indented statement is executed and X is incremented by 1. The DO WHILE is tested again. It is still true so X is again incremented. It loops 100 times, each time incrementing X by 1, until X = 100, after which time it moves on.

```
X = 0
DO WHILE X < 100
   X = X + 1
ENDDO
```

Loops may be nested. There must be an ENDDO for every DO WHILE. The following program simulates a clock (it does not keep real time, though). The outer loop (DO WHILE HOUR < 13) represents the hour and executes 12 times. The inner loop (DO WHILE MINUTE < 61) represents the minutes and executes 60 times for each time the outer loop executes once. Like the minute hand on a clock, the inner loop moves fastest and executes a total of 720 times.

PROGRAM 6.1   NESTED LOOPS

```
*CLOCK.PRG
*PROGRAM TO SIMULATE A CLOCK
CLEAR
HOUR = 1
*OUTER LOOP SIMULATES HOUR HAND
DO WHILE HOUR < 13
  @ 5, 10 SAY HOUR
  MINUTE = 1
  *INNER LOOP SIMULATES MINUTE HAND
  DO WHILE MINUTE < 61
    @ 6, 10 SAY MINUTE
    MINUTE = MINUTE + 1
  ENDDO
  HOUR = HOUR + 1
ENDDO
```

A Special Loop: DO WHILE .T.

This is an interesting use of the iterative structure. It looks like this in a program:

```
DO WHILE .T.
   .
   <commands>
   .
ENDDO
```

The literal interpretation is: "do while true." Do while what is true? Perhaps I can get a bit metaphysical for a moment and interpret it as "do everything between the DO WHILE and ENDDO so long as there is any truth in the universe." In other words, it is an endless loop; left to itself, it never quits looping.

Why have an endless loop in your program? It is usually used when you want processing to continue indefinitely *until some condition within the loop is reached,* after which an EXIT, RETURN, or QUIT causes the program to exit the loop. The usual construction is this:

```
DO WHILE .T.
   <commands>
   IF <condition>
     EXIT
   ENDIF
   <commands>
ENDDO
```

DO WHILE .T. is used many times in the sample programs throughout this book. Observe that there is always an IF and one of the unconditional or procedural branches (see below) somewhere within it.

Unconditional Branching Flow

There are two commands which cause unconditional branching. They are always used within DO WHILEs.

LOOP

This command causes program execution to jump immediately back to the beginning of the nearest DO WHILE. It is usually combined with an IF or DO CASE to skip past part of a loop:

```
DO WHILE . . .
   <statements>
   IF <condition>
    LOOP
   ENDIF
<statements>
   ENDDO
```

EXIT

EXIT causes execution to jump immediately *past* the ENDDO and out of the loop. Notice the difference between these important commands. LOOP goes back for another run through the loop while EXIT leaves the loop altogether. It, too, is usually used with IF or DO CASE.

Procedural Flow

Several commands cause program execution to transfer to another program, back to dBASE, or out of dBASE altogether.

DO <program name>

Causes execution to jump to another dBASE program. It may be used from the dot prompt or within a program to call another program into play.

RETURN

RETURN sends the program back to the calling program. If the program began at the dot prompt, this command returns to the dot prompt. If a program was called from another program, RETURN causes it to go back to the command immediately following the DO

<program name> in the calling program. I will cover subprograms in detail in chapter 12.

QUIT

This command immediately closes all files and returns to the operating system. This is the way to get out of dBASE.

RUN (or !)

Using either the word RUN or typing ! with a DOS command or program name executes the DOS command or runs a non-dBASE program. This has several uses:

- To execute a DOS command from within a program
- To run a separate non-dBASE program from within a program
- To execute a DOS command or other program from the dot prompt.

It is useful because dBASE's DOS-level file management commands are awkward and sometimes unreliable. For example, dBASE's DIR command does not have the flexibility of DOS's DIR command; I find it better to type !DIR to get the real DOS directory command with all its options.

7

Functions and Useful Programming Commands

This chapter builds upon the programming ideas of the previous chapter and shows how to use some functions and commands.

FUNCTIONS: BUILT-IN ROUTINES

Functions are a special type of statement that carry out complex manipulation of numbers, characters, and dates. They usually "return" a value. This means that the function goes off into the computer, does the calculation or manipulation, and returns with an answer, new string, or date. In truth, functions are little programs built into dBASE that save the programmer from having to work out common routines.

Most functions have two parts: the function name, and some data or expression to work on. They are always used with other verbs to display or use the results of the calculation or manipulation. The construction looks like this:

```
verb function(expn)
```

Before examining some functions let us see how to use them:

• The returned value is assigned to a variable on the left side of an equal sign. This example finds the square root of 456 and puts the answer in memory variable A:

```
A = SQRT(456)
```

or

```
STORE SQRT(456) TO A
```

- The returned value is displayed directly. This example displays the letters "American" on the screen:

```
MTITLE = "American Libraries"
? LEFT(MTITLE,7)
```

- The returned value is used as an expression in another function or command. This example combines the integer function with a LOCATE command to find a record in the database file in which salary is between $54367.00 and $54367.99:

```
LOCATE FOR INT(SALARY) = 54367
```

Function Types: Numeric

dBASE III+ is weak in numeric functions. dBASE IV has many more. They find square roots, absolute values, logarithms, maximums and minimums, integers, rounded off values, and the like. Here are the most useful ones (in all cases, expn may be a numerical constant, a variable storing a number, a numerical file field, or a mathematical expression):

```
INT(expn)
```
Converts a decimal number to an integer. It does not round—it just chops off the decimal part. See the example above.

```
ROUND(expn,n)
```

Rounds a decimal number to a specified number (n) of decimal places. A couple of examples:

```
? ROUND(250.7,0) displays 251
? ROUND(250.736,2) displays 250.74.
```

SQRT(expn) finds the square root of a number. See the example above.

```
MAX(expn,expn), MIN(expn,expn)
```

Finds the larger or smaller of two values. This example finds the larger of the values stored in A and B:

```
A = 120
B = 60
? MAX(A,B) displays 120.
```

STR(expn,n) converts n digits of a number to its equivalent characters. This function is important since numbers cannot usually be mixed into, combined, or used with other characters without first being converted. Some examples:

```
P = 7
? STR(P,1)   displays 7 (but this is the character "7" not
the number).
? STR(P,2)   displays 07.
```

Function Types: Character Manipulation

dBASE is rich in string functions that manipulate character data. They find substrings within strings of characters, find the first or last parts of strings, count the occurrence of specific characters, and so on. Like all functions, a string function returns a value that may then be displayed, put into a memory variable, or used with another command. I will describe a few now. Others will be included in the Serials System program examples. Unless otherwise noted, (expn) may be a quoted string, a variable or field containing a string, or a concatenation of these.

```
<expn> + <expn>
```

The plus sign used with characters concatenates. It sticks two strings together. This example shows how to use it when displaying names:

```
FIRSTNAME = "Doris"
LASTNAME = "Smith"
? FIRSTNAME + LASTNAME   displays DorisSmith
? FIRSTNAME + " " + LASTNAME displays Doris Smith.
? LASTNAME + ", " + FIRSTNAME displays Smith, Doris
```

UPPER(expn), LOWER(expn) changes all characters in the expression to upper or lower case:

```
MTITLE = "American Libraries"
? UPPER(MTITLE) displays AMERICAN LIBRARIES.
```

TRIM(expn) removes trailing spaces from an expression. It is used often to display fixed field data. Assume we have a personnel file that has a last name (LASTNAME) and first name (FIRSTNAME) of 20 characters each. Even though a particular employee's names may be short, the field still contains 20 characters, most of which are blank. The first example displays the data without trimming while the second example trims blanks off the first name:

```
(1) ? FIRSTNAME + LASTNAME
```

```
Doris               Smith
```

```
(2) ? TRIM(FIRSTNAME) + " " + LASTNAME
```

```
Doris Smith
```

SPACE(expn) creates a string with a specified number of spaces. (expn) must be a number. It can be used to put spaces in a field or variable, or to space output reports and displays.

```
MISSN = SPACE(9) puts 9 blank spaces in MISSN.
? SPACE(29) + "Anytown Public Library" displays the words
30 spaces from the left.
```

LEFT(expn,n), RIGHT(expn,n) extracts a specified number (n) of characters from the left or right part of a string. n may be a number or variable containing a number. Notice how they are used with a telephone number:

```
MPHONE = "716-811-2075"
? LEFT(MPHONE,3) displays 716
? RIGHT(MPHONE,8) displays 811-2075.
```

LEN(expn) gives the number of characters in a string:

```
? LEN(MPHONE)displays 12.
```

<expn> $ <expn> is the instring function. It checks to see whether a string of characters contains another string. If so, it returns a TRUE. I call it the "is contained in" function. Here is a simple, albeit not very typical, example to illustrate its use:

```
IF "John" $ "Johnson"
      ? "John is contained in Johnson"
ENDIF
```

The IF statement asks the computer to compare "John" with "Johnson." If the first string is contained in the second (which it is), the words following ? will be displayed.

A more typical example might be this one which asks the user to type a "keyword" from a journal title being sought. It searches the file for that word in the TITLE field:

```
ACCEPT "Enter any word from the title being soughtâ" TO
MGET
LOCATE FOR MGET $ TITLE
    .
    .
    .
```

You should read the above statement as "look through the database file searching in the TITLE field for any title that contains the words in MGET."

It is important to have the variables on the correct side of the $. If "John" and "Johnson" were reversed in the first example, the statement would not be true since "Johnson" is not contained in "John."

CHR(expn) changes an ASCII code into its equivalent character. (expn) must be a number from 1 to 255. This is useful when you need to display or print a character that is not on the keyboard. For example, ? CHR(5) will display . It is also used to send "control codes" to the printer. These are codes that cause the printer to underline, bold, italicize and so on. Chapter 12 gives some examples.

Function Types: Date

dBASE stores dates as numbers, making it possible to add, subtract, and compare dates. In addition, date functions derive the month name, day of week, and day of the month from a given date. Some important date functions are:

DATE() this function (with nothing between the parentheses) gives "today's date." This is the date entered when you boot the computer. It can be used by itself to display today's date, or combined with other date functions:

```
? DATE() displays today's date.
NDAYS = DATE() — OLDDATE places in memory variable NDAYS
the number of days between the date stored in OLDDATE and
today.
```

Several date functions return portions of a date, sometimes in numeric and sometimes in character form. (expn) must be a date of the form mm/dd/yy. In all the examples that follow, assume today's date is

December 18, 1990, and it has been stored in a memory variable called TODAY using the command: TODAY = DATE().

CDOW(expn) returns the day of the week spelled out:

```
? CDOW(TODAY) displays Tuesday.
```

MONTH(expn), YEAR(expn), DAY(expn) returns the numerical month, year, and day of a date:

```
? MONTH(TODAY)  displays 12.
? YEAR(TODAY) displays 1990.
? DAY(TODAY) displays 18.
```

CMONTH(expn) gives the calendar month:

```
? CMONTH(TODAY)  displays December.
```

A distinction must be made between a string of characters that resemble a date and a real date. Consider the following statements:

```
ADATE = "02/04/38"
BDATE = CTOD("02/04/38")
```

ADATE is a string of characters like any other. You can use string functions on it but not date functions. The CTOD function converts strings into real dates. BDATE is a real date that can be subtracted from another date to get the number of days between. It can be used with date functions, but not with string functions.

Function Types: Specialized Tests

Several special functions return only values of TRUE or FALSE. You use them to test the status of the database or of equipment. They are usually used in DO WHILE... and IF... structures. A few common ones follow. More illustrations of their use will be given in the next section. All of these have nothing between the parentheses:

EOF() returns TRUE if the pointer has reached the end of the file. We will see it in use in the sample programs to follow, but its usual construction is:

```
DO WHILE .NOT. EOF()
<statements>
ENDDO
```

or

```
IF EOF()
<statements>
ENDIF
```

FOUND() returns TRUE if a LOCATE found the desired record. It is usually used like this:

```
LOCATE FOR ISSN = MISSN
DO WHILE FOUND()
<statements>
ENDDO
```

DELETED() returns TRUE if a record has been marked for deletion. Database records may be marked for deletion but not actually taken out of the database. Until they are, they may be displayed, processed, or restored.

IIF(condition,expn1,expn2) is an interesting function that does not fall into any of the above categories. It returns one value if a condition is true and another if it is false. If the condition is true, it returns <expn1>, otherwise it returns <expn2>. The expressions may be characters, numbers, or dates. As an example, the following assigns the words "Gift" to MVEND if the vendor code is "G," and "Purchase" for any other value:

```
MVEND = IIF(VEND_CODE = 'G','Gift','Purchase')
```

It should be clear that this use of IIF is the same as the following:

```
IF VEND_CODE = 'G'
   MVEND = 'Gift'
ELSE
   MVEND = 'Purchase'
ENDIF
```

USER DEFINED FUNCTIONS

IV You may create your own functions in dBASE IV. They are called User Defined Functions, or UDFs. First, I will show the basic structure, followed by a simple example. The structure of a UDF is:

```
FUNCTION <name>
PARAMETERS <parameter list>
<commands>
RETURN(variable)
```

The UDF begins with the word FUNCTION followed by the function name. The PARAMETERS list provides input of data for the function to work on. The commands are normal dBASE commands to do the given task. The RETURN(variable) sends the new data back to the program. The program calls the UDF just like it would a normal function:

```
? <function name>(variable or value)
```

The following example takes the due date of a book, calculates the amount of fine owed (based on $.10/day), and returns to display the total fine:

```
**MAIN PROGRAM FRAGMENT
ACCEPT "Due date = " TO DUE
DUEDATE = CTOD(DUE)        && Converts to real date
? CALCFINES(DUEDATE)       && Calls function and prints results
.
********
**USER DEFINED FUNCTION
FUNCTION CALCFINES
PARAMETERS DUEDATE         && Receives DUEDATE from main program
OVERDUE = DATE() - DUEDATE && Calculates number of days
overdue
FINE = OVERDUE * .10       && Calculates fine
RETURN(FINE)               && Returns FINE to main program
```

USEFUL PROGRAMMING COMMANDS

We now examine in more detail a few of the several hundred dBASE commands, with examples of their use. Most commands have several options, expressions, scope statements, and conditions that make them flexible and useful for a wide range of programming tasks. I will not attempt to cover every option of every command but will concentrate on the most useful options for the Serials System. The dBASE manuals should be consulted to get the full range of commands and options available.

I wish to organize this section by placing commands into the following categories (some of these have already been discussed and some will be examined later):

Commands having to do with files:

- Creation of files
- Copying files
- Indexing and sorting

- Finding records
- Manipulating databases, setting relationships

Commands having to do with memory variables

- Creating memory variables
- Moving data around
- Functions

Commands having to do with input and output:

- Addition of data
- Editing of data
- Getting data from the keyboard
- Getting data from files
- Putting data into files
- Display and printing of data

Exclusive programming commands

- Flow structures

Environmental commands

- Controlling peripheral devices
- Parameter controls

Commands Having To Do With Files

You usually use Assist to create database file structures. You may also use the Interactive command: CREATE <file name>. CREATE cannot be used in programs, although if you have an existing database file, you can make another one with the programming command: COPY STRUCTURE TO <new name>. Usually systems designers create the structure of all database files before turning the programs over to the user.

Once a file has been created, a program may call it into play to:

- Add data
- Delete data
- Change data
- Search for data
- Combine its data with that of other files
- Copy its structure to create a new database file

Opening, Selecting, Closing Files
    USE, SELECT, CLOSE
    Before anything can be done to a file, it must be opened. Opening a file sets aside memory space called a buffer through which chunks of data move as they go from or to the file. Open database files with:

    USE <name>

where <name> is the name of the database file. A program would open BIB.DBF by including the command: USE BIB.
    Often it is useful to have several files open simultaneously, and dBASE allows you to have as many as ten database files open. dBASE III+ allows a total of 15 open files, including up to ten databases plus indexes, screen format instructions, subprograms, and so on. dBASE IV allows a total of 99 files to be open at the same time, but still only ten database files. Although several database files may be open, only one is considered active. The active one is the default—it is the one to which all commands are directed unless specified otherwise.
    The SELECT command, used in conjuction with USE, opens multiple files, as shown in the following example:

    SELECT 1
    USE BIB
    SELECT 2
    USE COPY

    SELECT numbers the file, and USE identifies the file by name. The last file SELECTed (in this example, COPY) is the active or default file. Any later references to a file or fields are assumed to refer to COPY. While COPY is active, references to BIB fields must be preceded by BIB-> (e.g., BIB->TITLE).
    If you wish to make BIB the active file, issue either of the following:

    SELECT BIB   or   SELECT 1

    BIB then becomes the default and you must use COPY-> to reference fields in that file (e.g., COPY->SUB_DATE). COPY.DBF may be made active again by either of the following:

    SELECT COPY   or   SELECT 2

    An important point: if in a program you place the command: USE BIB without the SELECT statement, BIB will be the *only* file open. A

USE without a SELECT closes all other database files and cancels previous SELECTs.

It is always a good idea to close files before exiting a program. Closing a database file writes data in the buffer to the file, updates certain file information, and fixes the disk directory. You may close databases in the following ways:

```
CLOSE <name>   or     CLOSE DATABASES
```

The first example closes the named file only (e.g., CLOSE BIB) while the second closes all database files.

Moving Around in Files

```
GOTO
```

Recall that dBASE uses a record pointer to indicate the "default" record—the one that will have action done to it unless specified otherwise. Some commands only change the pointer but take no further action; others change the pointer and do more visible things.

GOTO (or equivalently, GO) moves the record pointer to a particular record. It does not display or do anything to the record, just moves the pointer. You will use various other commands to display, change, or delete the record.

The command has three equivalent forms:

```
GOTO n
GO n
n
```

The record number, n, may be a number (GO 4), variable containing a number (GO M), or an arithmetic expression (GO M + 3). You also may use the words TOP (GO TOP) and BOTTOM (GO BOTTOM) which move the pointer to the first and last record.

SKIP is for times you may wish to move backward or forward through the file relative to the current record. SKIP does this:

```
SKIP [+] n
```

For example:

```
SKIP      Moves to the next record.

SKIP 5    Moves 5 records toward the end of the file,
          from the last one found.
```

```
SKIP -2    Moves back 2 records.
```

LOCATE is for when you wish to locate a certain record based on some criterion in the record itself. The following example uses a condition to move the record pointer:

```
LOCATE FOR TITLE = "American Libraries"
```

LOCATE finds the first record in the file that meets the condition. It only moves the record pointer. After locating the record, you may issue other commands to display, change, or delete it. This example finds the first record with this title (if one exists) and makes it the current record.

If there are no records with this title, the record pointer ends up past the last record on a spot called EOF (end of file). EOF is not the last record, it a marker past the last one.

Commands Having To Do With Memory Variables

dBASE has two places to get and put data: memory variables and file fields. Fields are permanent, named areas in a database file, which, taken together, make a data record. Memory variables (or simply, variables) are temporary storage areas in RAM that are given names by the programmer. Data coming from a file or keyboard for processing are stored in memory temporarily. A label or name is given to the data to identify it for subsequent processing.

Naming Variables
All data stored in memory must be given a name. The rules for naming variables are the same as for fields:

- Maximum of 10 characters
- Must begin with a letter
- Cannot have imbedded blanks
- May use letters, numbers, and the underscore (_). No other punctuation allowed.

Although it is not required, it is customary to begin memory variable names with the letter M, so as not to confuse them with file fields. Thus, a serial title field might be called TITLE, while the title data stored in a memory variable might be called MTITLE.

Types of Data in Variables
Variables may contain the same data types as fields (character, numeric, date, logical) except there is no memo type variable. Unlike fields where you had to specify their sizes and types ahead of time, variables sizes

and types are automatically determined by the data being placed in them. Placing character data into a variable makes it a character variable, placing a number makes it a numeric variable, and so on. Further, there are no rules about reserving certain names for certain types of data as there is in BASIC; there is nothing obvious about the spelling of the name that would suggest its type.

Arrays

IV An array is a group of memory variables storing related data. The variables have the same name, but numerical subscripts are used to distinguish individuals in the group. For example, suppose you needed to store all your vendor's names in memory at the same time. Instead of creating 10 or 12 separate memory variables, you could create one variable with 12 subscripts (e.g., VENDOR [1], VENDOR [2] . . . VENDOR [12]). The program would place data into, and take data out of, this array by reference to the subscript. Unfortunately, dBASE III+ does not support arrays,[1] but dBASE IV does.

Arrays are like tables. A one-dimensional array has only one column; arrays with two or more dimensions have multiple columns. Before storing data into an array, you must first declare some information about it:

```
DECLARE <name> [<number of rows>], [<number of columns>]
```

Using the above example of a single dimensional array (only rows, no columns), the command would be:

```
DECLARE VENDOR [12]
```

Any commands that move data to or from the array must use the appropriate subscript, for example:

```
? VENDOR [3]
```

The subscript can be a number, variable containing a number, or an arithmetic expression.

To follow this example one step further, suppose you had a file of vendor's names and addresses (VEND.BIB). The following fragment would read through the file and place the vendor's names and addresses into two arrays for further processing:

```
USE VEND
DECLARE VENDNAME [12]
DECLARE VENDADD [12]
```

```
I = 1
DO WHILE .NOT. EOF()
   VENDNAME [I] = VENDOR &&VENDOR is the name field
   VENDADD [I] = ADDRESS &&ADDRESS is the address field
   I = I + 1
   SKIP
ENDDO
   .
   .
```

Commands Having To Do With Input

This section will deal with simple input commands to get data into memory variables. Some of the same commands are also used to get and put data into database files.

Getting Data From the Program Itself
   = and STORE

Data may be placed into a variable directly by the program. These are called *constants,* and you place them there with the assignment statements: = and STORE. Here are a few examples that store constants into named memory variables:

```
MCOPY = 1              places a 1 in MCOPY
STORE 1 TO MCOPY       places a 1 in MCOPY
MISSN = '              stores 9 blank spaces in MISSN
MCLAIMDAYS = 30        stores the number 30 in MCLAIMDAYS
STORE 0 TO MCOST       makes MCOST equal to 0
```

You also may move data from one variable to another. Remember, this makes a copy of the data in the new place:

```
MCOPY2 = MCOPY
STORE MCLAIMDAYS TO MTEMP
```

Getting Data From the Keyboard
   ACCEPT, INPUT, WAIT

Several commands may be used to get data from the keyboard into memory variables. ACCEPT is most often used to enter character data into a memory variable. The usual construction is:

```
ACCEPT "<prompt>" TO var
```

The prompt is optional. If used, it is displayed on the screen and the program waits until the user types something at the keyboard. When **Return** is pressed, the data goes into variable, var. In the following example, whatever the user types goes into the memory variable MTITLE:

```
ACCEPT "Enter the Title" TO MTITLE
```

INPUT works the same as ACCEPT but is best for numeric data:

```
INPUT "Enter the subscription cost" TO MCOST
```

Another way to get data from the keyboard is with WAIT. Both ACCEPT and INPUT require that the incoming data be placed into a memory variable and the **Return** key pressed. WAIT differs in three ways:

- It takes only one character
- The *Enter* key is not required
- Storing the keystroke in a memory variable is optional.

It has a built-in prompt: "Press any key to continue..." In other words, the simplest form of WAIT is:

```
WAIT
```

This is often used to halt things so the user may read the screen and press a key when ready to move on. If you do not like the built-in prompt, you may substitute another. This example places a question on the screen and stores the answer in MCON:

```
WAIT "Do you wish to continue Y/N?" TO MCON
```

An important thing about ACCEPT, INPUT, and WAIT is that you cannot use them to get data from the keyboard and put it directly into a file. You must place the data into a memory variable first.

@...GET: gets data from the keyboard and places it either into a memory variable or directly into the file. I will explain its use with memory variables now, and with files later. The usual construction is:

```
var = expn
@ x,y GET var
AD
```

The x and y parameters are screen coordinates, row x and column y. The dBASE screen has 24 rows (lines), numbered from 0 to 23, and 80 columns, numbered from 0 to 79. The READ command highlights the designated position and places the cursor there waiting for the user to type some data. The highlight is as long as the data already in var. The entered data go into memory variable, var.

To use GET, var must be created beforehand by placing some data into it. You need a READ command to activate the GET. The following example first puts 20 spaces into MTITLE, moves the cursor to row 5, column 12, highlights the next 20 columns in row 5, and waits until you type something:

```
MTITLE = SPACE(20)
@ 5,12 GET MTITLE
READ
```

The column and row parameters may be absolute values, memory variables that contain values, arithmetic expressions, or any combination. Here are a few examples:

Absolute values	@ 5,1 GET...
Variables	@ A,B GET...
Expression	@ A+3,B GET...
Combination	@ 1,((80-LEN(TITLE))/2) GET...

Another form of GET uses the SAY command to place a prompt on the screen at the designated screen coordinates. The highlighted portion and cursor will immediately follow the quoted message:

```
MTITLE = SPACE(20)
@ 5,12 SAY "Please enter the serial title: " GET MTITLE
READ
```

One READ activates all GETs up to that point. If you have several GETS in a program, all the GETs are highlighted at the positions indicated, and the cursor jumps to the first one and waits. When you enter data and press **Return**, the cursor moves to the next highlight, and so on.

Following is a program fragment. Notice there is one READ for three GETs, and the variables are created before the GETs. When the program hits the READ, the quoted text is displayed at the screen locations indicated, followed on the same line by a highlight. The cursor will first be in the highlight for MISSN, awaiting input.

```
MISSN = SPACE(9)
MTITLE = SPACE(20)
MCOST = 0
@ 2,10m SAY "Enter ISSN: " GET MISSN
@ 5,8 SAY "Enter Title: " GET MTITLE
@ 7,10 Say "Enter Cost: " GET MCOST
READ
```

A powerful feature of GET is that it may be accompanied by "pictures" to make sure the user enters correct data types, of the correct length. The following example ensures that copy number is two numerical digits:

```
MCOPY = 1
@ 1,5 SAY "Enter Copy Number: " GET MCOPY PICTURE "99"
READ
```

The "99" means a two-digit number must be entered. Other data type pictures are:

PICTURE "AAAAA"	Allows only letters.
PICTURE "L"	Allows only logical data: upper and lower case T, F, Y, N (standing for true, false, yes, no)
PICTURE "#####"	Allows digits, blanks, and signs.

A RANGE statement also may be added to make sure numeric data fall within a certain range. The following example makes sure that the age of a prospective club member falls between 21 and 40:

```
AGE = 0
@1, 15 SAY "Enter applicant's age: " GET AGE RANGE 21,40
```

IV Validity checking using GETs has been enhanced in dBASE IV. Some useful new clauses are:

WHEN <condition>	Permits data entry only when a specified condition is met:

```
@ 4,0 GET LASTNAME WHEN AGE > 20
```

VALID <condition>	Causes an error message if the user attempts to enter the wrong kind

of data. This might be used in a
menu with choices from "A" to "I".
Any letter alphabetically after
"I" would be rejected:

```
@ 5,0 GET CHOICE VALID CHOICE < "J"
```

I will describe screen coordinates, GET, and SAY in more detail later. They become important in dealing with file fields since GET can be used to move data from the keyboard directly to a file without first going through a memory variable.

It is not a good idea to mix ACCEPTs (or INPUTs, WAITs) with GETs. Sometimes things do not turn out as you might wish. This is because GETs place the cursor at absolute positions and the others place it on the next line. Generally, I recommend that a single screen use either all GETs or combinations of ACCEPT/INPUT/WAIT.

Getting Data From a File
You can also use the assignment statements, (=) and STORE, to move data from a file field to a memory variable (a different command, REPLACE, is used to move data from a variable to the file).

A database must be opened and the desired record made the current record. This program fragment opens BIB.DBF, looks for the record with a specified ISSN (LOCATE . . .), and then places some field data into memory variables for subsequent processing:

```
USE BIB
ACCEPT "Which ISSN to search?" TO MISSN
LOCATE FOR ISSN = MISSN
MTITLE = TITLE
MFREQ = FREQ
MPUB = PUBLISHER
    .
    .
    .
```

Commands Having To Do With Output

The whole purpose of computer processing is to present meaningful information to the user. This section will further describe some ways to display data.

? The easiest way to display data is to use the question mark (?). The general form is:

```
? <expn>
```

where <expn> may be a quoted string, number, memory variable, file field, function, concatenation of these, or nothing (gives a blank line). The following examples illustrate:

```
String                  ? "Anytown Library"
Number                  ? 12
Memory variable         ? MISSN
Database field          ? TITLE
Concatenation           ? "Frequency: " + FREQ
Function                ? SQRT(4567.2)
Blank line              ?
```

The single question mark (?) displays data on the next line at the far left of the screen. In other words, ? gives a line feed and displays the contents of <expn>. Continuous use of ? causes the screen to scroll, moving information to the top of the screen and out of sight.

The double question mark (??) displays data at the present cursor position without first giving a line feed. Examples (1) and (2), below, are equivalent. Both display these lines on the screen:

```
Hello, Harry.
Welcome to the library.
```

```
1.    ? "Hello, " + FIRSTNAME + "."
      ? "Welcome to the library."
```

```
2.    ? "Hello, "
      ?? FIRSTNAME
      ?? "."
      ? "Welcome to the library."
```

Question marks give unformatted output. Screen design must be done by placing spaces within quotes, using concatenation (+), the space function, and ??. The following examples show three equivalent ways to place two menu items on one screen line:

```
Method 1:
? "        S = SEARCH FOR TITLES        A = ADD NEW TITLES"
```

```
Method 2:
? SPACE(7)+"S = SEARCH FOR TITLES"+SPACE(12)+"A = ADD NEW
TITLES"
```

```
Method 3:
```

```
? SPACE(7)+"A = SEARCH FOR TITLES"
?? SPACE(12)+"S = ADD NEW TITLES"
```

I introduced @...SAY in conjunction with GETs. This command may be used without GETs to display data at specific locations on the screen or printed page. The above menu could be modified as follows:

```
@ 2,8 SAY "1 = SEARCH FOR TITLES"
@ 2, 41 SAY "2 = ADD NEW TITLES"
```

@ ...SAY may display a character string, number, memory variable, database field, function, or concatenation of any of these. The screen coordinates may be numbers, variables containing numbers, or arithmetic expressions. Here are a few examples:

```
String              @ 5,1 SAY "Anytown Library"
Number              @ 5,1 SAY 12
Memory Variable     @ A,B SAY MISSN
Database Field      @ A+5,1 SAY TITLE.
Concatenation       @ 5,1 SAY "Frequency: " + FREQ
```

Commands To Control the Working Environment

The dBASE manual lists two kinds of "environmental commands": those which control peripheral devices, and those which set various parameters. The peripheral commands are CLEAR and EJECT. Their functions are similar, regarding the screen and printer, respectively. CLEAR clears the screen and places the cursor at the top left corner. EJECT ejects a page of paper from the printer and places the print head at the top of the new page.

dBASE III+ has over 50 commands to set various parameters which control how the computer responds to other commands and situations. dBASE IV has over 70. They all begin with the word SET. I will list a few to give an idea of what they do.

Most of the SET statements have "defaults." They are already set in certain ways when your program begins. If the defaults are acceptable, you need do nothing. Place in your programs only those that you want to change. In this list, I will give the non-default settings. Also note that a few of them end with TO . . . This means that TO must be followed by more words. What those additional words are depends on too many things to list here (I cover some throughout this book; consult the manual for the others).

SET BELL OFF	Turns off beeping noise during data entry (a good idea if you are working in a public area!)
SET CENTURY ON	Shows the century in date displays.
SET COLOR TO	Sets foreground, background, border colors.
SET CONFIRM OFF	Does not require carriage return during input.
SET DECIMALS TO	Determines number of decimals to display.
SET DEFAULT TO	Specifies default disk drive.
SET DEVICE TO SCREEN/PRINT	Specifies whether @...SAY will go to screen or printer.
SET ESCAPE OFF	Disables Escape key.
SET EXACT ON	Requires exact matches in character comparisons.
SET FORMAT TO	Opens a custom screen for data entry.
SET INDEX TO	Opens index files.
SET MARGIN TO	Sets left margin of a printer.
SET PRINT ON	Sends output to the printer.
SET PROCEDURE TO	Opens a procedure file.
SET RELATION TO	Links two databases on a common field.
SET TALK OFF	Does not echo commands on the screen.

Once you have SET a parameter, it remains that way until another SET statement changes it, or you quit dBASE. This can be a problem if one of your programs sets a parameter that is not wanted in another program. Be sure to set parameters back to their defaults.

IV Besides the SET statements, dBASE IV has some 25 powerful "system memory variables," which are used mostly to format displayed output. For example, you can use them to set the length of printed pages, print the date and page number at various positions on reports, set printer pitch, set word wrap, set amount of indent in new paragraphs, and so on.

Endnotes

1. Desperate dBASE III programmers had to make up for this severe loss by using "pseudo-arrays," in which similar variable names were given numerical suffixes to relate them. See L. Castro, J. Hansen, and T. Rettig, *Advanced Programmer's Guide*. (Culver City, Calif.: Ashton-Tate, 1985), pp. 239-243.

8

Screen Design, Data Input, and Display

Data input and screen design go hand in hand, and this chapter will show how to design screens to input and display database data. As usual, dBASE gives several options:

- Using screen format commands in programs.
- "Painting" a screen with dBASE's screen generator.
- Using dBASE's default screen.

The last option permits no design at all. I call it the "quick and dirty method." It has its uses and I will describe it later in this chapter, although I recommend using the first two options in combination to create customized, user-oriented data input screens that present a clear, uncluttered, prompted interface to the user. Customized screens give instructions to the user, allow validity checks, and lead the user through the steps of the process, making data entry as comfortable and efficient as possible.

An organization adds database records throughout the life of the system, often by different people, at different times, under different circumstances. Most databases grow a little at a time, usually in spurts. The usual pattern is to start with a large retrospective conversion followed by somewhat slower maintenance activity. Data input in a complete system should be a regular menu function.

PROGRAMMING AN INPUT SCREEN

There are several dBASE commands used in screen design. They are:

- Commands to place data, instructions, and prompts on the screen:

  ```
  ?
  ??
  @...SAY
  TEXT
  ```

- Commands to get data from the keyboard:

  ```
  @...GET
  ACCEPT
  INPUT
  ```

- Commands to clear the screen:

  ```
  CLEAR
  @...CLEAR
  @...CLEAR TO...
  ```

- Commands to draw lines and boxes and change colors:

  ```
  @...TO...
  @...TO...DOUBLE
  SET COLOR TO...
  ```

- Various functions:

  ```
  + (concatenation)
  SPACE(expn)
  TRIM(expn)
  LEFT(expn)
  STR(expn)
  ROW()
  COL()
  ```

I covered most of these commands and functions in chapter 7. This section will concentrate on some that have not yet been mentioned and extend the use of others to screen design.

Using TEXT...ENDTEXT

The TEXT command is a handy way to display blocks of textual material. Everything between the words TEXT and ENDTEXT will be displayed exactly as typed in the program. Indents and blank lines will be preserved. The following example clears the screen and then displays a short menu:

```
CLEAR
TEXT
            Anytown Public Library
            Anytown, New York
            Serials Control System

1 = ADD RECORDS        2 = CHANGE RECORDS
3 = DELETE RECORDS     4 = RETRIEVE SELECTED RECORDS
0 = QUIT PROGRAM

ENDTEXT
ACCEPT "Enter desired function" TO CHOICE
  .
  .
```

TEXT...ENDTEXT only displays textual material. It cannot be used to display file data. Nor can you place any input commands between TEXT and ENDTEXT. Notice where the input command ACCEPT is placed in the above example.

Clearing the Screen

A significant part of screen design is knowing when and how to clear old information from the screen to make room for new. CLEAR is used in various ways to clear different parts of the screen. Used by itself, the word CLEAR wipes all information from the screen and places the cursor at the top left corner.

To clear part of a screen, use one of the following forms:

```
Form:                  Examples:
a x,y CLEAR            (1) a 5,0 CLEAR
                       (2) a 16,20 CLEAR
a a,b CLEAR TO c, d    (3) a 12,30 CLEAR TO 18,50
                       (4) a 12,30 CLEAR TO 12,70
```

The first form clears from row/column coordinates x,y down to the bottom right corner. In Example (1), it clears the entire bottom portion of the screen from line 5 down. This comes in handy when you wish to clear information off the screen but leave a header at the top. Example (2) clears the bottom right corner from line 16, column 20; everything else remains on the screen.

The second form clears a rectangular space anywhere on the screen, from upper left coordinates a,b to lower right coordinates c,d. Example (3) clears a window in the approximate center of the screen. This is not really a window as it does not save the information "under the window."

It just clears a box so you can place something new there. Example (4) clears part of one line, from column 30 to 70, by using identical line coordinates.

dBASE IV Windows

IV dBASE III lacks true windowing capabilities, but dBASE IV has ten commands to make, save, edit, and move windows. Windows are treated as little screens that can be saved and recalled with the data in them and behind them kept intact.

The most important dBASE IV commands for using windows are:

```
DEFINE WINDOW <name> FROM a,b TO c,d
```

This defines and saves a window rectangle from screen coordinates a,b to c,d. You also can add parameters to show the kind of border and colors desired.

ACTIVATE WINDOW <name> activates the named window. All screen operations, including @...SAYs and GETs, are relative to the window borders (instead of the usual top left corner of the screen) and all screen output goes to the window.

DEACTIVATE WINDOW <name> deactivates the named window and restores the screen to its previous state.

Lines and Boxes

If used sparingly, lines and boxes make for spiffy screens. The syntax is:

```
@ a,b TO c,d
@ a,b TO c,d DOUBLE
```

The first set of coordinates (a,b) pinpoints the location of the top left corner of the box; the second set (c,d,) defines the bottom right corner. The word DOUBLE draws a double line box. Following are a few examples:

@ 5,0 TO 10,79	Draws a single line rectangle from row 5, column 0 to row 10, column 79.
@ 5,0 TO 10,79 DOUBLE	Draws a double line rectangle.
@ 5,0 TO 5, 79 DOUBLE	Draws a double horizontal line from column 0 to 79 on line 5.
@ 5, 10 TO 20, 10	Draws a single vertical line down column 10 from row 5 to row 20.

Boxes do not get along well with ACCEPT, INPUT, WAIT and some ?s. If you try to use these within a box, you will surely mess it up. Use SAY and GET inside boxes.

Lines and boxes may not print on some printers. Some printers must be set up to enable them to print such graphics. Chapter 12 describes some techniques for printing graphics.

Two additional functions, ROW() and COL(), are useful. They return the current screen line and column, and may be used as the parameters in SAY statements. For example:

ⓐ ROW(), 5 SAY...	Displays on the current line (at the point where the previous display stopped), starting in column 5.
ⓐ ROW() +2, 1 SAY...	Skips two screen lines before displaying the data at column 1.
ⓐ 10, COL() +1 SAY...	Displays on line 10 one column to the right of the previous display.

The ROW() function may be used in IF statements to test whether you are getting too close to the bottom of the screen. The following program fragment moves through the file from beginning to end, continually displaying serial data, one line at a time. When it has gone past line 20, it pauses and asks the user to press a key to continue. The CLEAR command clears the screen, sets ROW() back to 0, and displays the next serial at the top of the screen.

```
DO WHILE .NOT. EOF()
  ? ISSN + " " + TRIM(TITLE) + " " + FREQ + " " + PUBLISHER
  IF ROW() > 20
    WAIT
    CLEAR
  ENDIF
  SKIP
ENDDO
```

"PAINTING" AN INPUT SCREEN

It can be a lot of bother coming up with screen locations for SAYs and GETs. However, dBASE has a facility for "painting" a custom input screen. The process creates a "format file (.FMT)" that contains the SAYs and GETs. You can use the format file in two ways: your program can call it like a subprogram when you want to use the screen, or you can use the painting process to give you SAY and GET locations that you then rewrite into your program.

I have given the name BIB.FMT to the input screen for addding new records to BIB.DBF. The screen may be used to add new records, display selected records, and change records.

Painting a screen is easier to do than describe. I will show how to get started. If you need more help, several texts[1] give a complete tutorial, and the dBASE manuals cover the process in detail.

You start the adventure with:

```
dBASE III+ Assist Mode:
Create/Format/Enter the name of the file: BIB
Set up/Select database file: C:BIB
Set up/Load Fields
```

At this point the fields from BIB appear on the screen. Choose the ones you wish to have in the screen (here, all of them), then hit **F10** to move them around. Move them by placing the cursor inside the field highlight, pressing **Return**, moving to where you want it to be, and pressing **Return** again. It is important to know that you are moving the field input areas, not the field names. Field names stay in the upper left corner to be erased eventually. You may type any other text and add graphics. There is a menu item for making single- and double-line rectangles.

IV dBASE IV uses the following menu items to get a similar, but more flexible, screen paint module:

```
dBASE IV Control Center:
Form/<create>/Quick Layout
```

Figure 8.1 shows the custom input screen. It resembles a form. Prompts are customized and meaningful. Instructions are included, as are code meanings. The user is not aware of file names, field names, or field types. The structure of the database file is invisible. He or she only has the impresson of filling out a form.

FIGURE 8.1 Custom Input Screen

```
                        ANYTOWN LIBRARY
                     SERIALS CONTROL SYSTEM
                      DATA INPUT & CHANGE
 ┌──────────────────────────────────────────────────────────────┐
 │  ISSN: 0002-9769      Title: American Libraries               │
 │                                                               │
 │  Frequency: M    Publisher: American Library Association      │
 │   ┌──────────────────────────────────────────────────────┐    │
 │   │  Frequency codes: D = Daily; W = Weekly; BW = Biweekly;│   │
 │   │    M = Monthly; Q = Quarterly; I = Irregular; A = Annual│  │
 │   └──────────────────────────────────────────────────────┘    │
 │                                                               │
 │  Volumes per year: 12  Issues per numbered volume:  1         │
 ├───────────────────────────────────────────────────────────────┤
 │                                                               │
 │   ┌──────────────────────────────────────────┐                │
 │   │  Exit anytime with <Ctrl> <End>          │                │
 │   └──────────────────────────────────────────┘                │
 └──────────────────────────────────────────────────────────────┘
```

ADDING DATA WITH THE CUSTOM SCREEN

The following program fragment shows how to "call" the screen. The important commands for using a custom screen are marked with &&:

```
USE BIB
CON = "Y"
DO WHILE UPPER(CON) = "Y"
   SET FORMAT TO BIB      &&this calls the screen
   APPEND BLANK
   READ                   &&this puts it on the monitor
   SET FORMAT TO          &&this releases the screen
   ACCEPT "Do you wish to continue Y/N?" TO CON
ENDDO
CLOSE DATABASES
QUIT
```

SET FORMAT TO BIB opens BIB.FMT. However, the screen does not appear until the READ statement is hit. Before that, APPEND BLANK adds a new blank record to the end of the file, awaiting data. When it hits READ, the screen appears and you may type data into the screen and directly to the file. Use the arrow keys to move back and forth between highlighted areas, and hit **Return** to move to the next highlight. So long as you have not finished adding data to the last (bottom) highlight, you can move around the screen at will, making changes.

The program must hit APPEND BLANK and READ for every record added. To do this, put these commands inside a DO WHILE loop. Then there must be a way to quit. In the above fragment, the loop continues until the user types something other than "Y" to the question about continuing.

Even if you are finished with the screen, it is still active and "waiting in the wings." It will reappear anytime a READ is hit anywhere in the program. This may not be desirable, so the screen should be deactivated by issuing:

```
SET FORMAT TO
```

In fact, it is not a bad idea to bracket the READ statement as shown in the above fragment turning the screen on and off with each pass through the loop.

You can use the same screen and commands to display and change existing records. In this case do *not* use APPEND BLANK. Instead, use a routine to search for the record to be displayed or changed, followed by READ. See chapter 12 for search techniques.

PROBLEMS WITH CUSTOM SCREENS

Although custom input screens are easy to create using the screen paint facility, there are some problems at least in dBASE III+):

1. You can only input data into one file with a single screen, and it is difficult to have more than one screen visible simultaneously. Program 8.1, below, uses two files but the program must jump between two screens.
2. In dBASE III+, you cannot make conditional judgments between GETs. Often, you may wish to input data only if certain conditions exist and skip them otherwise. At other times, you would like to evaluate data before entering other data. You cannot do these things with a customized screen, although dBASE IV has corrected some of the problems.

Most programs will use a combination of painted screens and separate SAY, GET, ACCEPT, INPUT, WAIT statements. The painted screen is best for routine input operations, while the individual program statements are best when you need more flexibility (for example, when you need to use pictures, range statements, conditional input, and so on). Separate program statements are also best for inputting non-file data in response to prompts, questions, and the like.

ADDING DATA WITH ASSIST

Although I recommend using custom screens, you can input data through Assist. Assist should only be used when you, the system designer, are also the person responsible for inputting data. It also may be used during program development to add a few records to test your programs. It uses the standard screen shown in Figure 8.2. Field names are used as prompts, placed in the top left corner of the screen in their order on the file. There are no specific input instructions, and it is esthetically unpleasant. It is generally not acceptable for user-oriented systems.

FIGURE 8.2 Quick and Dirty Input Screen

```
Record No.          1
ISSN           ABCD
TITLE          TITLE ABCD
FREQ           M
PUBLISHER      PUBLISHER ABCD
NOS_VOL        1
VOL_YR         2
```

To add records, choose the following menu options:

```
dBASE III+ Assist Mode:
Set Up/Database file/C:(the drive that contains the data
                            files)
Enter the name of the file: BIB
Update/Append

dBASE IV Control Center:
Data/BIB
F2
```

Type in the data, one field at a time. Use the arrow keys to move around among the fields. The **Return** key moves the cursor to the next field down the screen. If you fill the field with data, the cursor automatically moves to the next field. Hit **PgDn** to go to the next record. You can hit **PgUp** to move into a previous record to correct mistakes or add missing data. Hit **Ctrl End** to quit and save the data.

PROGRAM TO ADD SERIAL DATA

The following program includes two painted screens, one for BIB.DBF and one for COPY.DBF, as well as other screen input and display statements. It may be used to add a completely new serial, add additional copies, change existing data, or finish partially entered records. You first enter the ISSN and the program searches for it in BIB. If found, it displays the record on the screen so you can change data. If not found, you get a blank form to add data. You may optionally go to the copy data input screen.

PROGRAM 8.1 SERADD.PRG ADD Serial Data

```
 1 *SERADD.PRG
 2 *PROGRAM TO ADD SERIALS
 3 *BIBLIOGRAPHIC DATA
 4 *USES BIB.FMT AS INPUT SCREEN
 5 *USES COPY.FMT IF COPY DATA ADDED
 6 SET TALK OFF
 7 SELECT 1
 8 USE BIB INDEX ISSNDEX
 9 SELECT 2
10 USE COPY INDEX ISSNCOP
11 SELECT 1
12 *START MAIN LOOP
```

```
13    DO WHILE .T.
14    CLEAR
15    @  1, 33  SAY "ANYTOWN LIBRARY"
16    @  2, 29  SAY "SERIALS CONTROL SYSTEM"
17    @  3, 35  SAY "DATA INPUT"
18    @ 4,5 TO 4,75 DOUBLE
19    MISSN = SPACE(9)
20    @  5,  5  SAY "ISSN (Blank to Quit):" GET MISSN
21    READ
22    IF LEN(TRIM(MISSN)) = 0
23      CLOSE DATABASES
24      RETURN
25    ENDIF
26    SEEK MISSN
27    IF EOF()
28     APPEND BLANK
29     REPLACE ISSN WITH MISSN
30    ENDIF
31    *WHETHER ISSN IS FOUND OR NOT
32    *ACTIVATE INPUT SCREEN BIB.FMT
33    SET FORMAT TO BIB
34    READ
35    SET FORMAT TO
36    COPYGO = 'Y'
37    @ 15,3 CLEAR TO 18,74
38    @ 15,3 SAY 'Do you wish to add copy data Y/N?' GET COPYGO
39    READ
40    IF UPPER(COPYGO) = 'Y'
41     MCOPY = 1
42     @ 16,3 SAY 'Copy Number to Add:' GET MCOPY PICTURE '99'
43     READ
44     SELECT 2
45     SEEK MISSN + STR(MCOPY,2)
46     IF EOF()
47       APPEND BLANK
48       REPLACE ISSN WITH MISSN, COPY WITH MCOPY
49     ENDIF
50     SET FORMAT TO COPY
51     READ
52     SET FORMAT TO
53    ENDIF
54    SELECT 1
55  ENDDO
```

NOTES ABOUT SERADD.PRG

This program has four major parts:

1. Set the environment and open files, lines 1-11.
2. Ask user for ISSN and search BIB for it. If not found, add blank record (APPEND BLANK), lines 13-30.
3. Activate BIB.FMT for data entry, lines 33-34.
4. Repeat process for Copy data, lines 35-55.

Lines 1-5: Comments
Lines beginning with * are comments that are ignored by the interpreter. Place comments anywhere in a program as a form of documentation:

```
*SERADD.PRG
*PROGRAM TO ADD SERIALS
*BIBLIOGRAPHIC DATA
```

Line 6: SET TALK OFF
This environmental control command tells the computer not to echo program commands on the screen. It should be at the beginning of all programs. Otherwise, your screens will be a mess.

Lines 7-11: SELECT, USE
These lines open files and their corresponding indexes and make BIB the "active" file:

```
SELECT 1
USE BIB INDEX ISSNDEX
SELECT 2
USE COPY INDEX ISSNCOP
SELECT 1
```

Lines 19-21: Asking for ISSN to Start
Although most of the input screen instructions are in BIB.FMT it is necessary first to ask for the ISSN before activating the custom screen:

```
MISSN = SPACE(9)
@ 5, 5 SAY "ISSN (Blank to Quit):" GET MISSN
READ
```

Lines 22-25: Testing for Blank Data
This program has a continuous loop to add serials continuously (DO WHILE .T.). To stop, leave the ISSN blank. If MISSN is blank, it returns to the main menu:

```
IF LEN(TRIM(MISSN)) = 0
  CLOSE DATABASES
  RETURN
ENDIF
```

The literal interpretation of this routine is: "if the length of the data in MISSN, trimmed of blanks, is 0, then CLOSE DATABASES and RETURN to the menu."

Line 26: Index Search
SEEK MISSN searches the index for the value stored in MISSN. Chapter 12 goes into more detail about how to search with indexed files.

Lines 27-30: Testing for End of File
EOF() is a function that returns a TRUE if the record pointer is at the bottom of the file. If this happens, it means the SEEK was unsuccessful. In this program, you want to add a blank record (APPEND BLANK) if the ISSN does not already exist in the file. If the search was successful, do not add a record:

```
IF EOF()
  APPEND BLANK
  REPLACE ISSN WITH MISSN
ENDIF
```

Lines 29, 48: Replacing File Fields
There are two ways to change data in a file field. One is GET, the other is REPLACE. GET places or changes field data directly, while REPLACE places or changes field data with data generated elsewhere in the program. Notice in Line 48 that data stored in memory variable MISSN moves into the file field ISSN, and data from MCOPY goes into COPY:

```
IF EOF()
  APPEND BLANK
  REPLACE ISSN WITH MISSN, COPY WITH MCOPY
ENDIF
```

Lines 33-35: Activating Input Screen
Line 33 sets the format to BIB.FMT and Line 34 gives the READ. At this point, execution of the program halts and the screen takes over. Line 35 deactivates the screen when the user either fills the form or hits Ctrl End:

```
SET FORMAT TO BIB
READ
SET FORMAT TO
```

Line 40: UPPER Function
Lines 36-40 ask if the user wishes to add copy data. Line 40 uses the
UPPER function to permit the user to type either uppercase or lowercase
responses. The routine uses GET, making READ necessary:

```
COPYGO = 'Y'
@ 15, 3 CLEAR TO 18,74
@ 15, 3 'Do yu wish to add copy data Y/N?' GET COPYGO
READ
IF UPPER(COPYGO) = 'Y'
  .
  .
```

Lines 42-45: Adding Copy Data
Before adding copy data, Line 42 asks which copy number to add. The
program defaults to copy 1. Line 44 makes COPY.DBF the active file,
and Line 45 searches it for the combination of ISSN and Copy number:

```
MCOPY = 1
@ 16, 3 SAY 'Copy Number to Add:' GET MCOPY PICTURE '99'
READ
SELECT 2
SEEK MISSN + STR(MCOPY,2)
IF EOF()
  APPEND BLANK
  REPLACE ISSN WITH MISSN, COPY WITH MCOPY
ENDIF
SET FORMAT TO COPY
READ
SET FORMAT TO
```

Again, if it does not find that particular ISSN/Copy on the file, the
program adds a blank record. If found, it displays the data, on the
assumption that either the user made a mistake or wishes to change
something.

Lines 50-51 activate the copy input screen. It is shown in Figure 8.3:

ADDING RECORDS TO MREC.DBF

Information is added to BIB.DBF and COPY.DBF only when new
serials or additional copies are added to the collection. These are stable
files with low activity and volatility.

FIGURE 8.3   Copy Input Screen

```
                        ANYTOWN LIBRARY
                     SERIALS CONTROL SYSTEM
                     COPY INPUT & CHANGE

    ISSN: 0002-9769   Title: American Libraries

    Copy Number:  1

    Cost: $   50.00    Vendor: D     Subscription Due Date: 09/01/91
                     ┌──────────────────────────────────────┐
                     │ Vendor codes: D = Direct; M = McGregor;│
                     │               F = Faxon;  O = Other    │
                     └──────────────────────────────────────┘
    Cover Date, First Received Issue:    06/01/89
    Cover Volume, First Received Issue:   20

    To add a note, move cursor here --> memo
            and press <Ctrl> <PgUp>
```

Not so with check-in data that are added often, probably daily. The check-in program should be optimized for speed. One way to speed things up is not to display bibliographic information or old check-in data. Just have the user enter the check-in information directly.

On the other hand, the check-in clerk may wish to review the previous check-in data. The price for this is more complicated programming and slower check-in. The main menu has both options. This method, while not as efficient, presents some interesting programming possibilities. The process is too dynamic and complex to use a painted input screen so I place the screen instructions right in the program.

A control program, called CHECKIN.PRG (see Program 8.2), asks for the ISSN. It also allows title searches if you do not know the ISSN. Depending on the frequency, it calls one of three programs to do the actual check-in (Lines 37-44).

PROGRAM 8.2   CHECKIN.PRG Control Program for Check-in

```
 1  *CHECKIN.PRG
 2  *MAIN PROGRAM FOR SERIALS CHECK-IN
 3  *SEARCHES ISSN
 4  *CALLS MCHECK.PRG, WCHECK.PRG, DCHECK.PRG, DEPENDING
 5  *ON FREQUENCY
 6  SET TALK OFF
 7  MISSN = SPACE(9)
 8  DO WHILE .T.
 9    CLEAR
10    @  1, 33 SAY "ANYTOWN LIBRARY"
11    @  2, 29 SAY "SERIALS CONTROL SYSTEM"
```

```
12    @  3, 35  SAY "DATA INPUT"
13    @ 4,1 TO 4,79 DOUBLE
14    MISSN = SPACE(9)
15    @  5, 5 SAY "ISSN (Blank to Quit):" GET MISSN
16    @  6, 5 SAY "Enter a <T> for Title search if ISSN not known"
17    READ
18    IF LEN(TRIM(MISSN)) = 0
19      CLOSE DATABASES
20      RETURN
21    ENDIF
22    IF UPPER(MISSN) = "T"
23      DO SRCH
24      LOOP
25    ENDIF
26    USE BIB INDEX ISSNDEX
27    SEEK MISSN
28    IF EOF()
29      @ 21,1 SAY 'That periodical not found'
30      @ 22,1 SAY 'Enter another ISSN, T, or <RETURN> to Quit'
31      WAIT
32      LOOP
33    ENDIF
34    MTITLE = TITLE
35    MCOPY = 1
36    MYR = STR(YEAR(DATE()),4)
37    DO CASE
38      CASE FREQ = 'D'
39        DO DCHECK
40      CASE FREQ = 'W' .OR. FREQ = 'BW'
41        DO WCHECK
42      OTHERWISE
43        DO MCHECK
44    ENDCASE
45 ENDDO
```

Program 8.3 is the subprogram for checking monthly periodicals. Programs for checking weekly and daily periodicals are similar except they show one month's worth of data on the screen instead of one year.

PROGRAM 8.3 MCHECK.PRG Review and Check-in of Monthly Serials

---

```
1 *PROGRAM: MCHECK.PRG
2 *SUBPROGRAM  FOR CHECKING IN
3 *MONTHLY, 6/YR, QUARTERLY, IRREGULAR MAGAZINES.
4 *CALLED BY CHECKIN.PRG AFTER TITLE IS FOUND
```

```
 5    USE MREC INDEX MREC
 6    a 5,37 SAY "Copy:" GET MCOPY PICTURE '99'
 7    a 5,48 SAY "Year:" GET MYR
 8    READ
 9    KEY = MISSN + STR(MCOPY,2)+MYR
10    SEEK KEY
11    IF EOF()
12      a 21,1 SAY "That Copy not found."
13      WAIT
14      LOOP
15    ENDIF
16    a 5,0 CLEAR TO 9, 79
17    a 5,1 SAY 'ISSN: ' +MISSN+' Copy: '
18    a 5,22 SAY MCOPY PICTURE '99'
19    a 5, 26 SAY 'Title: ' + MTITLE
20    a 6,1 TO 6, 79 DOUBLE
21    a 7,0 SAY MYR+'                '
22    a 7,10 SAY ' 1       2       3       4       5       6'
23    a 8,10 SAY 'JAN     FEB     MAR     APR     MAY     JUN'
24    a 14,10 SAY ' 7       8       9       10      11      12'
25    a 15,10 SAY 'JUL     AUG     SEP     OCT     NOV     DEC'
26    a 9,0 SAY 'VOL:'
27    a 10,0 SAY 'ISSUE:'
28    a 11,0 SAY 'ACTION:'
29    a 12,0 SAY 'DATE:'
30    a 16,0 SAY 'VOL:'
31    a 17,0 SAY 'ISSUE:'
32    a 18,0 SAY 'ACTION:'
33    a 19,0 SAY 'DATE:'
34    DO WHILE YR=MYR .AND. ISSN = MISSN
35      M = VAL(MON)
36      IF  M < 7
37        X =  M*9
38        a 9,X SAY VOL
39        a 10,X SAY ISSUE
40        a 11,X+3 SAY ACTION
41        a 12,X SAY TOD
42      ELSE
43        X =  (M-6)*9
44        a 16,X SAY VOL
45        a 17,X SAY ISSUE
46        a 18,X+3 SAY ACTION
47        a 19,X SAY TOD
48      ENDIF
```

```
49     SKIP
50   ENDDO while yr = myr
51   M = MONTH(DATE())
52   DO WHILE .T.
53     @ 23,0 SAY "Which month to change or add?"
54     @ 23,30 SAY "Enter month NUMBER or 0 to stop ";
55     GET M PICTURE '99' RANGE 0,12
56     READ
57     IF M = 0
58      RETURN
59     ENDIF
60     SEEK KEY + STR(M,2)
61     IF EOF()
62       APPEND BLANK
63     ENDIF
64     IF M < 7
65       X =  M*9
66       @ 9,X GET VOL PICTURE '9999'
67       @ 10,X GET ISSUE PICTURE '9999'
68       @ 11,X+3 GET ACTION PICTURE '!'
69       @ 12,X GET TOD
70     ELSE
71       X =  (M-6)*9
72       @ 16,X GET VOL PICTURE '9999'
73       @ 17,X GET ISSUE PICTURE '9999'
74       @ 18,X+3 GET ACTION PICTURE '!'
75       @ 19,X GET TOD
76     ENDIF m < 7
77     READ
78     REPLACE ISSN WITH MISSN, COPY WITH MCOPY, YR WITH MYR
79     REPLACE MON WITH STR(M,2)
80   ENDDO
81   *END OF PROGRAM MCHECK.PRG
```

NOTES ON MCHECK.PRG

This program has five major sections:

1. Open the file, ask for the copy number and year, and search the file for it, lines 5-15.
2. Place a calendar on the screen, lines 16-33.
3. Place data from the file into the calendar, lines 34-50.
4. Ask for the month number and append a blank record, lines 51-63.
5. Input new check-in data, lines 64-79.

Lines 34-50: Converting Month Number to Screen Position
This routine pulls one year's worth of check-in data for one serial off the
database and converts each check-in month number to a screen column
location, X. The statements, @ 9,X SAY VOL, etc., use X to place the file
check-in data into a calendar:

```
DO WHILE YR=MYR .AND. ISSN = MISSN
M = VAL(MON)
IF  M < 7
  X =  M*9
  @ 9,X SAY VOL
  @ 10,X SAY ISSUE
      .
ELSE
  X =  (M-6)*9
  @ 16,X SAY VOL
      .
ENDIF
SKIP
ENDDO while yr = myr
```

Lines 64-76: Adding Check-in Data
The user enters the month number of the issue to be checked in. The
routine in Lines 64-76, which is similar to that in Lines 36-48, places a
highlight in the correct calendar position. The user enters the *Volume*
and *Issue numbers, Action code,* and the *check-in* date:

```
IF M < 7
  X =  M*9
  @ 9, X GET VOL PICTURE '9999'
      .
ELSE
  X =  (M-6)*9
  @ 16, X GET VOL PICTURE '9999'
      .
ENDIF m < 7
READ
```

The Action codes are:

    R—issue received.
    F—issue not received and a first claim should be sent.
    S—issue not received and a second claim should be sent.
    B—is or should be bound.

The user remains in this program until 0 is entered as the month number, after which it returns to CHECKIN.PRG (Lines 57-59). This moves somewhat faster than it takes to describe, but it still takes time to place the calendar on the screen, read the data from the file, and place it in the calendar.

Lines 78-79: Placing Check-in Data on the File
The GETs in the Lines 66-75 move data directly from the keyboard to the file. The REPLACE command in Lines 78-79 use data that have been generated earlier and places them in appropriate fields:

```
REPLACE ISSN WITH MISSN, COPY WITH MCOPY, YR WITH MYR
REPLACE MON WITH STR(M,2)
```

Endnotes

1. George Tsu-der Chou. *dBASE III Plus Handbook*. 2nd ed. (Indianapolis: Que Corporation, 1986); *Using dBASE IV* (Carmel, Indiana: Que Corporation, 1990).

9

Sorting and Indexing

Sorting and indexing are among the most important processing functions. People usually enter database records into the file in no particular order. New serials are added to the end of the database as they arrive, and, as a result, even if the database started out in alphabetical order, it quickly becomes disordered.

There is a tendency to insert new records in their proper alphabetical place within the database. Resist the temptation. A computer file is not a card file. It is best not to worry about order until it comes time to process output. Then, ad hoc orderings can be made to meet specific reporting needs.

Sorting and indexing are used to order a database file. Although there are similarities between them, the results, techniques, and purposes differ.

SORTING

Sorting takes an existing file and creates a new one with the records in order by some designated field or fields. You use the second file in all respects like any other. You may sort on any field except the memo field. Character fields are sorted in alphabetical order, numeric fields in numeric order, and date fields in chronological order. The general structure is:

```
USE <database name>
SORT ON <field> TO <sorted database name>
```

For example, the following commands will sort a file of names and addresses (NAME.DBF) on LASTNAME and create a new file called SNAME.DBF:

```
USE NAME
SORT ON LASTNAME TO SNAME
```

Multi-level Sorts

You may sort on more than one field, in which case the program sorts on the first field until it finds a duplicate, then it sorts the duplicates on a second field, and so on. Each field to be sorted is named in the command, in priority order. To include first names in the above sort, issue this command:

```
SORT ON LASTNAME, FIRSTNAME TO SNAME
```

Sorting Part of a Database File

Unless specified otherwise, SORT copies all the records in the original file to the new one. You may limit the number of records transferred. The following example transfers and sorts only five records:

```
SORT ON LASTNAME, FIRSTNAME TO SNAME  NEXT 5
```

The next example transfers and sorts only those records that contain the indicated zip code. It sorts on last name, then on age in descending order for those with the same last name:

```
SORT ON LASTNAME, AGE/D TO SNAME FOR ZIP = '14260'
```

The sorting command of dBASE is flexible and easy to use, enabling you to sort the same file in different ways to meet different needs. Each sort creates a new file that takes up as much disk space as the original (providing you have sorted all records).

IV dBASE III+ sorts character fields in "computer order" where "Z" comes before "a" (A. . .Za. .z). IV has corrected this serious problem by adding a "dictionary sort" option. This sort method is case insensitive and sorts in this order: Aa. . .Zz.

An important caveat: the new file has no continuing association with the original. This is especially important. Additions, deletions, or changes in one will not automatically add, delete, or change data in the other. Records added to SNAME after sorting it are placed on the end, like any other database. New records are not automatically placed in alphabetical order. Finally, sorting is a slow process. A large database file can take several minutes to sort.

You can use Assist to sort a database file. To sort BIB.DBF on the PUBLISHER field and create a sorted file called BIBPUB.DBF, choose these menu options:

```
dBASE III+ Assist Mode:
Set Up\Database File\C:BIB.DBF
                Is the file indexed? N
Organize\Sort\PUBLISHER
            Enter a file name . . .BIBPUB.DBF


dBASE IV Control Center:
Data\BIB\Modify structure/order
            Sort database\Shift-F1 (to choose fields to sort)
                PUBLISHER
                Enter name of sorted file: BIBPUB
```

The following commands issued at the dot prompt or placed in a program do the same thing:

```
USE BIB
SORT ON PUBLISHER TO BIBPUB
```

INDEXING

Indexing also retains the original order of the database file but instead of creating a new file, it creates a smaller index file with pointers to the original. The index is not a separate database file; you use it only with the main database. Besides ordering the database, indexing provides for very fast search and retrieval.

dBASE III+ and IV differ in how they handle indexes. Everything explained here will work in both versions, but I will explain several powerful new dBASE IV options at the end of this section.

Creating the Index

First, let us index BIB.DBF on the PUBLISHER field using Assist:

```
dBASE III+ Assist Mode:
Set Up\Database File\B:BIB.DBF
                Is the file indexed? N
Organize\Index\The index key  . . .PUBLISHER
        C:
        Enter the name of the file: PUBDEX.NDX
```

This creates an index by PUBLISHER called PUBDEX.NDX that may only be used with BIB.DBF. The equivalent commands, used at the dot prompt or in programs, are:

```
USE BIB
INDEX ON PUBLISHER TO PUBDEX
```

Multi-Field Indexing

Multi-field indexing is similar to that described for multi-level sorting. Sometimes the goal of multi-field indexing is to make a unique key for each record. For example, referring again to the name and address file, you may wish to index NAME.DBF on LASTNAME and FIRSTNAME. The following command does it:

```
INDEX ON TRIM(LASTNAME) + ", " + FIRSTNAME TO NAMEDEX
```

The word TRIM trims off trailing blanks from LASTNAME while the "+" joins the last and first names with a comma and space between. If you could look into it, the index file would look like this:

```
AKER, RALPH          4
BROWN, ALICE         3
BROWN, MARY          2
JONES, GERRY         5
JONES, HARRY         1
etc.
```

The first column is a string of characters concatenated from LASTNAME and FIRSTNAME. This string would be used to search the index. The second column is the record number of the associated record in NAME.DBF.

COPY.DBF uses multi-field indexing to obtain unique keys. Since a library may own several copies of the same serial, neither the ISSN nor copy number alone are unique. To make an index with a unique key for each copy of each serial, it is necessary to combine the ISSN with Copy number:

```
INDEX ON ISSN + STR(COPY,2) TO ISSNCOP
```

Because COPY is a numeric field, it must be converted to characters before combining it with ISSN. The STR(COPY,2) function temporarily converts 2 numeric digits in COPY to equivalent characters (in essence, the number 7 becomes "07").

Sometimes it is necessary to combine many fields in the index to come up with a unique key. MREC.DBF requires complex indexing because only the combination of ISSN + COPY # + year + month results in a unique key for check-in data. The command to create its index is:

```
INDEX ON ISSN + STR(COPY,2) + YR + MON TO MREC
```

Multiple-Index Files

Applications such as the Serials System may use several indexes for one database file. For example, BIB.DBF should be created and maintained in no particular order, but you need three indexes to make full use of it: ISSNDEX (by ISSN), TITLEDEX (by TITLE), and PUBDEX (by PUBLISHER).

The following commands placed in a program or issued from the dot prompt create these indexes:

```
USE BIB
INDEX ON ISSN TO ISSNDEX
INDEX ON TITLE TO TITLEDEX
INDEX ON PUBLISHER TO PUBDEX
```

Indexing Empty Database Files

An interesting thing about dBASE is that you do not need records in a file to index it. All you need is a structure. You can issue the above commands on an empty file. Later, when you add records to the file, the system automatically adds appropriate data to the indexes. By contrast, the sort command sorts only those records residing in the file at the time.

This feature comes in handy in programming. You can create all the database files and indexes "outside the program," using the Assist Mode if desired. This makes for faster, less error-prone program operation. Only rarely is it necessary to index a file within a program.

Using Indexes

The INDEX ON. . . command creates an index to a database file. The index will be by one or more fields. You may give the index any legitimate DOS name you choose, and dBASE adds an extension of .NDX to distinguish it from a database file.

To use an index with a file, follow the USE statement with the word INDEX and the index name:

```
USE BIB INDEX ISSNDEX
```

Regardless of how the file itself is arranged, it will now seem to be arranged in ISSN order in all subsequent listings or searches.

Just as important, any additions or deletions to BIB.DBF will update ISSNDEX.NDX automatically. I should add that failure to include the index in the USE statement will ruin the index if additions or deletions are made to the database file. You must then reindex or create a new index. If you plan to make changes to the database, it is most important that indexes be included in the USE statement.

What if you have more than one index for a database? You should include all of them in the USE statement. Maintenance of BIB.DBF might use the following command:

```
USE BIB INDEX TITLEDEX, PUBDEX, ISSNDEX
```

Any additions or deletions to BIB automatically updates all three indexes. However, if you *retrieve* from BIB, only the first named index, TITLEDEX, is the "controlling" index. The file appears to be arranged by title. If you wanted it to be arranged by publisher, you would use the following:

```
SET INDEX TO PUBDEX, TITLEDEX, ISSNDEX
```

This keeps the others open for updating but makes PUBDEX the controlling one.

Indexing With dBASE IV

IV dBASE IV has an additional indexing option. Instead of creating several separate indexes to one database, you may create one "multiple index file (.MDX)," which may contain up to 47 index tags or fields for a single database. Any of the tags in the multiple index file may be used to impose order on the database. The multiple index file will usually have the same name as the database file but with an .MDX extension. There are two ways to create the .MDX file: during database creation, by answering Y to the question about whether each field should be indexed; by issuing the following command at the dot prompt or in a program:

```
INDEX ON <key expression> TO TAG <tag name>
```

<key expression> is a field or concatenation of fields, the same as in III+, <tag name> is any name of ten characters or less by which you will later identify the controlling index order. The BIB example would look like this:

```
USE BIB
INDEX ON PUBLISHER TO TAG PUBDEX
INDEX ON TITLE TO TAG TITLEDEX
INDEX ON ISSN TO TAG ISSNDEX
```

The name of the resulting index would be BIB.MDX and its tags would be PUBDEX, TITLEDEX, and ISSNDEX, respectively.

To specify one of the tags to be the controlling index use this command:

```
USE BIB ORDER TITLEDEX
```

or:

```
SET ORDER TO TITLEDEX
```

The use of tags and the .MDX file cleans up the messy problem of having to keep track of numerous index files. More importantly, it always opens and updates the .MDX whenever the database is opened. I recommend using tags if you are using IV.

Again, I wish to emphasize that the dBASE III+ indexing commands, outlined at the beginning of this section, will work in DBASE IV. Programs written for III+ can be migrated to IV with no changes. It is important to remember, however, that it is not a two-way street; these new IV commands will not work in III+.

Indexing Advantages and Disadvantages

You may make as many indexes on as many fields as needed. The indexes usually do not take up as much disk space as the original and they are updated with the main database file when you add, change, or delete records.

The disadvantage of indexing is that it is not as flexible as sorting. You must index the entire file; there is no conditional indexing. You must use certain additional commands to call an index into play and some indexing options are a bit awkward. Still, knowledgeable use of these commands and options regains lost flexibility, and then some. In sum, it seems better to index than sort for most applications. Chapter 11 examines how to get serials information out of indexed databases.

10

Relating Files

The idea behind a relational database is to avoid putting all your eggs (records) into one basket (file). A relational database manager, like dBASE, can take separate files and relate them so information seems to be coming from a single file.

Here are some ways in which Serials System files might be related:

- Printing claim letters. A claim letter may require the ISSN and title data from BIB, check-in data from MREC, and publishers' addresses from PUB. Printing a letter requires data from three files.
- Displaying complete bibliographic data on the check-in screen. You must link at least two files: BIB and either MREC, WREC, or DREC.
- Printing an expiration alert list. A complete list should include ISSN, title, vendor, publisher, cost, subscription date. Some of these data are in BIB and some in COPY.

WAYS OF RELATING FILES

The most common methods of relating files are:

- Joining two files to create a third.
- Updating a master file from a transaction file.
- Moving between files during processing.
- Establishing a direct correspondence between the record pointers of two files.

Joining Two Files to Create a Third

The JOIN command merges specified records from two files to create a new file containing the combined data. For example, you might wish to create a new file to hold the title, copy, year, and month of all monthly periodicals that have an "F" in the ACTION field (indicating that a first notice should be sent). Because the title comes from BIB and the rest from MREC, you need data from both. The newly created file would then be used to print a claim list.

The programming or dot prompt commands are:

```
SELECT 1
USE BIB
SELECT 2
USE MREC
JOIN WITH BIB TO CLAIMS FOR ISSN = BIB->ISSN;
.AND. ACTION = "F" FIELDS BIB->TITLE, COPY, YR, MON
```

MREC (the active file) is joined with BIB to create CLAIMS.DBF for those periodicals that have a common ISSN in both files (ISSN = BIB->ISSN) *and* for which there is an "F" in the ACTION field of MREC. The FIELDS . . . statement lists the fields to be included in CLAIMS. The arrow (->) means the field (i.e., TITLE) comes from BIB instead of MREC. The rest of the data comes from MREC.

Figure 10.1 illustrates the effect of the above command. CLAIMS can now be used as a normal database file. You can sort or index it, use it to search for and display records, print a claims list, print claim letters, and so on.

FIGURE 10.1   JOIN Illustration

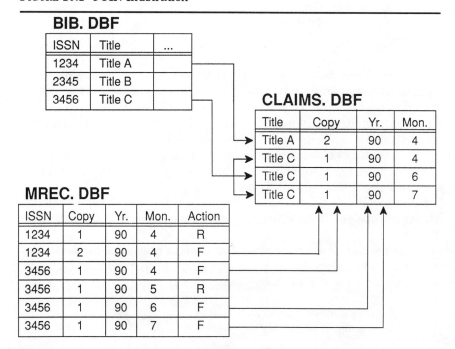

JOIN is best for those applications which use the third file (here, CLAIMS.DBF) in a batch mode, and in which you, the programmer, know which data will be needed for it. It is therefore best for printing lists, form letters, or displaying large portions of the database.

Updating a Master File From a Transaction File

Some applications lend themselves to "transaction file processing." This means that data are collected in a temporary file and, periodically, the collected data are used to update a permanent master file.

As an example, suppose the Serials System had a file of account data (I will call it ACCOUNTS.DBF). A field in it holds an account number and is called ACCTNO. Another field, ACCTBAL, stores the account balance. All purchases are gathered in a transaction file called TRANS.DBF. It has only two fields, ACCTNO and AMT. Once per month, TRANS is run against ACCOUNTS reducing the account balances in the latter by the amounts in AMT.

The following commands cause each account in ACCOUNTS to be reduced by the purchases to that account in TRANS. Figure 10.2 illustrates the process:

```
SELECT 1
USE TRANS
SELECT 2
USE ACCOUNTS
UPDATE ON ACCTNO FROM TRANS REPLACE ACCTBAL WITH;
ACCTBAL - TRANS->AMT
```

UPDATE is useful when the application lends itself to maintaining a permanent master database while collecting transactions in a temporary file. It should be used only in those applications in which you do not need an up-to-the-minute master file. For example, it could be used for circulation control, keeping daily circulations in a transaction file which is then run against the master file at night. The problem is that the master file is not reliably up-to-date throughout the day, precluding inquiries about status.

Moving Between Two Files During Processing

This method is effective when you need to process data from more than one file in a more dynamic situation than JOIN or UPDATE allows. It usually involves the following steps:

1. Finding a needed record in one file.
2. Displaying or processing data from it.

3. Storing some key data in a variable.
4. Switching to the other file (using SELECT).
5. Searching the new file for the key data.
6. Displaying or processing data from the new file.

FIGURE 10.2 UPDATE Illustration

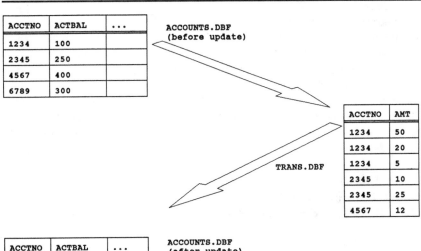

Program 10.1 prints a list of periodicals due to expire within a designated number of months. It switches between BIB and COPY to retrieve appropriate data from each.

PROGRAM 10.1 EXPALERT.PRG Expiration Alert

```
1   *PROGRAM EXPALERT.PRG
2   *THIS PROGRAM PROVIDES LISTINGS OF PERIODICALS
3   *DUE TO EXPIRE WITHIN SO MANY DESIGNATED MONTHS
4   *IT MOVES BETWEEN TWO DATABASES
5   SET TALK OFF
6   SELECT 1
7   USE BIB INDEX ISSNDEX
8   SELECT 2
9   USE COPY INDEX ISSNCOP
10  AMONTH = 6
```

```
11  CLEAR
12  a  1, 33   SAY "ANYTOWN LIBRARY"
13  a  2, 29   SAY "SERIALS CONTROL SYSTEM"
14  a  3, 32  SAY "EXPIRATION ALERT"
15  a 4,1 TO 4,79 DOUBLE
16  a 6,1 SAY "For how many months in advance do you wish to be
        alerted?" GET;
17  AMONTH PICTURE '99'
18  READ
19  ADATE = INT(AMONTH*30.4)
20  WAIT "Press any key when printer ready..."
21  SET PRINT ON
22  ? "Exp. Date ISSN    Copy Number          Title"
23  ? "   Vendor       Publisher                 Cost"
24  ?"-----------------------------------------------------------"
25  ??"----------------"
26  ?
27  LINECOUNT = 4
28  DO WHILE .NOT. EOF()
29    IF SUB_DATE - DATE() < ADATE
30      MISSN = ISSN
31      MVEND = VEND_CODE
32      MCOST = COST
33      ?  "  " + DTOC(SUB_DATE)+" " +ISSN + " "
34      ?? COPY
35      SELECT 1
36      SEEK MISSN
37      ?? "         " + TITLE
38      ? "         " + MVEND + "     " + PUBLISHER + "  $"
39      ?? MCOST
40      LINECOUNT = LINECOUNT + 2
41      IF LINECOUNT > 60
42        EJECT
43        LINECOUNT = 1
44      ENDIF
45      SELECT 2
46      SKIP
47    ELSE
48      SKIP
49    ENDIF
50  ENDDO
51  ?
52  SET PRINT OFF
53  RETURN
```

NOTES ABOUT EXPALERT.PRG

This program lists serials due to expire within a specified number of months. It searches through COPY looking for serials due to expire. When it finds one, it prints TITLE and PUBLISHER from BIB.DBF and all other data from COPY.DBF. It has five major sections:

1. Open files and display heading, lines 1-15.
2. Ask for number of months to be alerted, calculate the number of days from it, lines 16-19.
3. Print heading on printer, lines 20-26.
4. Conduct sequential search in COPY looking for serials due to expire and print copy data, lines 28-34.
5. Switch to BIB to print bibliographic data, lines 35-50.

Lines 16-19: Expiration Date Alert Calculation
This routine asks the user for the number of months of advance notice. AMONTH holds the number. Line 19 is a formula to convert the month number into the number of days between now and then. ADATE stores the number of days:

```
a 6, 1 SAY "For how many months in advance do you wish to
be alerted?" GET AMONTH PICTURE '99'
   READ
   ADATE = INT(AMONTH*30.4)
```

Lines 28-50: Testing for Expiring Serials—Switching Database Files
This is the heart of the program. These commands illustrate the technique of opening a file, displaying some data, switching to another file and retrieving a related record. It is a loop that looks through all records in COPY.DBF. If the subscription date is within the alert period (Line 29) data are printed from COPY:

```
DO WHILE .NOT. EOF()
IF SUB_DATE - DATE() < ADATE
      MISSN = ISSN
      MVEND = VEND_CODE
      MCOST = COST
      <print data from COPY>
      SELECT 1
      SEEK MISSN
      <print data from BIB>
```

While in COPY, critical data are stored in memory variables.

We now switch to BIB and SEEK the same ISSN. Data are then printed from BIB.

```
          SELECT 2
          SKIP
          ELSE
          SKIP
    ENDIF
    ENDDO
```

We now switch back to COPY and SKIP to the next record in it. If the subscription date is not within the alert period, the program jumps from Line 28 to Line 47 and skips to the next record in COPY. It then moves to the top of the loop (Line 27) to start over.

Lines 27, 40-44: Counting the Lines

It is a good idea to count the number of lines printed to allow for a bottom margin. Line 26 sets a counter (LINECOUNT) to 4, and Line 40 increments it by 2 for each serial printed. When more than 60 lines have been printed, it ejects the paper and sets the counter back to 1:

```
LINECOUNT = LINECOUNT + 2
IF LINECOUNT > 60
   EJECT
   LINECOUNT = 1
ENDIF
```

It would be a good idea to reprint the headings on the new page, in which case Lines 22-26 should be duplicated after Line 42.

Setting a Relation Between Two Files

SET RELATION is a powerful command that links data in two files based on a common field. One file is the parent; the other is the child. When you search the parent or otherwise move the record pointer, a corresponding movement is made in the child. This provides the most dynamic linkages; it is almost as if you were working with only one file.

For example, the following statements make COPY.DBF the parent and BIB.DBF the child (this is backward from the hierarchical examples given earlier—the beauty of a relational database is that structures are not rigid). The relationship is set from COPY to BIB based on their common ISSN field. The two files will always be aligned according to ISSN:

```
SELECT 1
USE BIB INDEX ISSNDEX
SELECT 2
USE COPY INDEX ISSNCOP
SET RELATION TO ISSN INTO BIB
```

If you search for a particular ISSN in COPY, the same ISSN will be found automatically in BIB. The requirements are (1) both files must have a field with the same name, and (2) the child file must be indexed on that field.

To break the relationship, use:

```
SET RELATION TO
```

with nothing following the TO.

PROGRAM 10.2 Illustrates the use of SET RELATION:

```
 1  *PROGRAM EXP2.PRG
 2  *THIS PROGRAM PROVIDES LISTINGS OF PERIODICALS
 3  *DUE TO EXPIRE WITHIN SO MANY DESIGNATED MONTHS
 4  *USES SET RELATION
 5  SET TALK OFF
 6  SELECT 1
 7  USE BIB INDEX ISSNDEX
 8  SELECT 2
 9  USE COPY INDEX ISSNCOP
10  SET RELATION TO ISSN INTO BIB
11  AMONTH = 6
12  CLEAR
13  @  1, 33  SAY "ANYTOWN LIBRARY"
14  @  2, 29  SAY "SERIALS CONTROL SYSTEM"
15  @  3, 32  SAY "EXPIRATION ALERT"
16  @ 4,1 TO 4,79 DOUBLE
17  @ 6,1 SAY "For how many months in advance do you wish to be alerted?";
18  GET AMONTH PICTURE '99'
19  READ
20  ADATE = INT(AMONTH*30.4)
21  WAIT "Press any key when printer ready..."
22  SET PRINT ON
23  ? "Exp. Date ISSN     Copy Number            Title"
24  ? "   Vendor        Publisher                    Cost"
25  ?"-------------------------------------------------------------"
26  ??"---------------"
27  ?
28  LINECOUNT = 4
29  DO WHILE .NOT. EOF()
30    IF SUB_DATE - DATE() < ADATE
31       ?  "  " + DTOC(SUB_DATE)+" " +ISSN + " "
32       ?? COPY
```

```
33     ?? "          " + BIB->TITLE
34     ? "          " + VEND_CODE + "     " + BIB->PUBLISHER + "  $"
35     ?? COST
36     LINECOUNT = LINECOUNT + 2
37     IF LINECOUNT > 60
38        EJECT
39        LINECOUNT = 1
40     ENDIF
41     SKIP
42   ELSE
43        SKIP
44   ENDIF
45 ENDDO
46 ?
47 SET PRINT OFF
48 RETURN
```

NOTES ON PROGRAM 10.2

This is the same program as Program 10.1 except that it makes use of SET RELATION (Line 10) instead of switching back and forth between the two files:

```
SELECT 1
USE BIB INDEX ISSNDEX
SELECT 2
USE COPY INDEX ISSNCOP
SET RELATION TO ISSN INTO BIB
```

As the program moves through COPY (Lines 29-45), it automatically moves BIB's record pointer to the same ISSN. The print statements (Lines 31-35) are a bit different because COPY remains the active database file. Fields printed from BIB must be preceded by BIB->:

```
?? "          " + BIB->TITLE
? "          " + VEND_CODE + "     " + BIB->PUBLISHER + "  $"
```

A serious limitation of SET RELATION in DBASE III+ is that you may relate only two files (in formal terms, a parent may have only one child). A relation can be set from COPY to BIB but it may not also be set from COPY to another file simultaneously.

However, a parent can have a grandchild. That is, though a second relation cannot be made from COPY to another file, a relation can be made from BIB to another file.

DBASE IV ENHANCEMENTS FOR RELATING FILES

IV dBASE IV has corrected the problem described in the last paragraph. It now allows a parent file to be related to any number of child files, providing they have common fields.

Many of the enhancements in dBASE IV revolve around better commands for relating files. You can use its SQL language to create sets of data (called relations) from several files. Those relations can be searched, displayed, and manipulated like files. You may even save them.

There are powerful new commands that selectively retrieve data from several files, sort, and display the results, as if only one file is involved. Other commands allow you to correlate data in several files to form the basis for retrieval.

In addition, IV has improved the menu system and screen painting modules to allow Assist manipulation of more than one file simultaneously. This is a major improvement over III+.

11

Finding, Presenting, and Deleting Records

Chapter 8 described simple but inelegant ways to add data to a database file. It also described more powerful, flexible methods based on programming. This chapter will also show both simple and complex methods of finding, displaying, and reporting information, and it will conclude with a discussion of deleting records.

FINDING RECORDS

Finding and displaying information go hand in hand. Following are some different ways of finding records in the database file.

Finding Records by Record Number

Recall that GOTO (or equivalently, GO) moves the record pointer to a particular record. It does not display or do anything to the record, just moves to it.

Generally, GO is not very useful in programming. Sometimes it is used to find your way back to a particular record after you have moved elsewhere in the file, or moved to a different file and back. Suppose you locate a record in BIB and display some of it. Then, for whatever reason, you move the record pointer. Later, you wish to return to the original record for more processing. The following routine uses the function RECNO() to store the current record number in a variable. Later, the program uses this variable to GO to the original record:

```
USE BIB
LOCATE FOR TITLE = "American Libraries"
<display or process this record>
N = RECNO()
DISPLAY FOR FREQ = "M"   &&This changes the record pointer
GO N                     &&This puts it back
<do further processing>
```

Finding Records Which Meet Conditions

Finding records in which one of the fields meets a condition is a powerful way to retrieve records from the database file. The condition may be any of those described in chapter 6. The command to do it is:

```
LOCATE FOR/WHILE <field> <operator> <value>
```

The value on the left of the operator always refers to a file field; the value on the right may refer to a field, variable, constant, or expression. Again, LOCATE only moves the record pointer to the first record which meets the condition. After locating the record, you would issue commands to display, change, or delete it.

The example below finds and displays some data from the first record (in BIB) with the title "American Libraries". It then stores the ISSN into the memory variable MISSN, goes to COPY and displays data from the first record with the same ISSN:

```
USE BIB
LOCATE FOR TITLE = "American Libraries"
? ISSN + " " + TITLE + PUBLISHER
MISSN = ISSN
USE COPY
LOCATE FOR ISSN = MISSN
? COPY
? COST
 .
 .
```

To find the next record that meets the same criteria use:

```
CONTINUE
```

CONTINUE operates differently depending on whether it follows a LOCATE FOR or a LOCATE WHILE. Following a LOCATE FOR, it finds the next record meeting the criteria regardless of how many other records intervene. Following a LOCATE WHILE, it quits searching when it hits the first record not meeting the criteria.

There is a special loop that can be used with LOCATE. It is:

```
DO WHILE FOUND()
  .
  .
ENDDO
```

To illustrate, the following program fragment finds and displays the ISSN, copy number, and subscription due date of *all* records with a particular vendor code:

```
USE COPY
ACCEPT "Enter Vendor Code (M, F, D, O):" TO VEN PICTURE '!'
LOCATE FOR VEND_CODE = VEN
DO WHILE FOUND()
  ? ISSN + "     " + STR(COPY,2) + "     " + DTOC(SUB_DATE)
  CONTINUE
ENDDO
```

Incidentally, STR and DTOC temporarily change copy number and subscription date, respectively, to character strings. These functions are necessary because you cannot combine numbers and dates with characters without first converting them. Also, PICTURE '!' changes the inputted code to upper case to match the upper case codes on the file.

You may use LOCATE to find records in either an unindexed or indexed file. The LOCATE command is powerful but slow.

Finding Specific Records in an Indexed File

SEEK, on the other hand, is fast. SEEK requires two conditions for it to work: the file must be indexed on the field(s) to be searched; the index must be activated by the USE statement. The syntax is:

```
SEEK <expn>
```

The expression, <expn>, may be a string, number, memory variable, date, or concatenation. Here are two examples:

```
SEEK "Pierian Press"
SEEK MTITLE
```

The first of the above examples assumes that the database file is indexed by publisher; the second by title. You can only SEEK the indexed field. If a file is indexed only on ISSN, you cannot SEEK it by title (you can LOCATE by either field).

The expression is not a condition. Notice that there is no field name and no operator. You are searching for a match between <expn> and the index key, so field names and operators are not used. The following is *incorrect*: SEEK PUBLISHER = "Pierian Press".

SEEK comes up with the first record that matches <expn>. To move to the next record use SKIP. It moves to the next record in the index regardless of whether or not it matches <expn>.

There is nothing equivalent to CONTINUE or DO WHILE FOUND() for finding subsequent records after SEEK. All records with the same key value will be next to each other in the index, anyway. Once the first record is found, conduct a sequential search until the key value changes. The following program fragment illustrates how to do this:

```
USE BIB INDEX ISSNDEX
ACCEPT "Enter ISSN of desired serial: " TO MISSN
SEEK MISSN
DO WHILE ISSN = MISSN .AND. .NOT. EOF()
   <display or process records>
   SKIP
ENDDO
```

SEEK MISSN finds the first record with the desired ISSN. The loop goes through the index until either the ISSN changes or it reaches the end of the file. SKIP moves through the index one record at a time. You would display, print, or do something with the records between the DO WHILE and the SKIP.

It is easy to confuse CONTINUE and SKIP. Use CONTINUE *only* after LOCATE. It finds the next record in the file, or the index if one is active, *that meets the search criteria*. You cannot use CONTINUE after SEEK. Use SKIP after either LOCATE or SEEK. It goes to the next record in the file or index, *regardless of the search criteria*.

Sequential Access of the Entire File

dBASE uses random file organization but that does not mean you must always do random searches. Often, you need to go through the entire file sequentially from beginning to end. For example:

• The database is sorted or indexed and you wish to list all records in it in order. If the database is sorted or indexed (and the index is open), sequential listings will be in the order of the sort or index.

- The order of the records does not matter but you need a listing of the entire database.
- You need a listing of the data in the order in which they were added to the database (chronological order).

I will illustrate this process in the sample programs that follow. The general construction for doing sequential access is:

```
DO WHILE .NOT. EOF()
    .
    .
    .
    SKIP
ENDDO
```


DISPLAYING AND PRINTING INFORMATION

Simple Displays

We have seen that there are simple and complex ways to add data to a database file. Likewise, there are simple and complex ways to display data. Assist provides a simple way to examine the contents of a database file. It is useful during program development and testing. Choose the following options from the Assist menu:

```
dBASE III+ Assist Mode:
Set Up\Database file\B:
        Enter the name of the file: BIB
Retrieve\Display\Specify scope\All
        Execute the command

dBASE IV Control Center:
Data\BIB
     Use file
Data\BIB
     Display records
```

This displays all the data in BIB—all fields and all records. If there is not enough room on one line, the data wraps around to the next line. It is a very sloppy display.

You do not have to display every record. By adding search conditions and scopes, you may display only records that meet certain criteria. dBASE III+ and dBASE IV use very different Assist and Control Center methods for doing this (programming methods are the same—I will discuss programming methods later in this chapter). This section will show how to use Assist to build a search condition. The next section will describe dBASE IV's "query by example" method.

You may choose **Build a search condition** to limit the records to be displayed. Choose the field to which the condition should apply, and then type the condition.

For example, to display only records in which the publisher is Prentice-Hall, choose the following from the Assist menu:

```
dBASE III+ Assist Mode:
Retrieve\Display\Build a search condition
              PUBLISHER
              = Equal To\"Prentice-Hall"
        Execute the command
```

There is also a "Specify scope" option with which you may display only the current record (**Default scope**), a specified number of records (**NEXT n**), a particular record (**RECORD n**), or the rest of the file (**REST**):

```
Retrieve\Display\Specify scope\NEXT 5
        Execute the command
```

Conditions and scopes can be specified through dot commands. Here are a few examples which should be self-evident:

```
USE BIB
DISPLAY NEXT 5
DISPLAY RECORD 6
DISPLAY REST
DISPLAY ALL
DISPLAY FOR PUBLISHER = "Prentice Hall"
```

IV dBASE IV uses "query by example" (QBE) to search for records that meet particular criteria. QBE means that a *file skeleton* is placed on the screen. The skeleton shows the database fields, and you type the desired criteria in the column under the field name. For example, to search BIB.DBF for serials published by Prentice Hall, you would type "Prentice Hall" in the column labeled PUBLISHER. To search COPY.DBF for serials costing more than $100, you would type >100 in the COST field.

To get into QBE from the Control Center, type the following sequence of commands:

```
dBASE IV Control Center:
Data/BIB
Query/<create
Use Tab to move to PUBLISHER column and type: "PRENTICE
HALL"
F2
```

Formatted Displays and Reports

The methods just described give unformatted displays: data are presented on the screen in the same order and format as on the file. They are not very useful in user-oriented systems. On the other hand, programming can create useful, informative reports that are user-centered instead of computer-centered. Here are some possible improvements:

- Displaying only specified records instead of the entire file. Programming provides much more flexibility than Assist or DIS-PLAY in choosing data.
- Displaying records from more than one file. Using programming, you can combine bits and pieces of data from several databases on one screen or printout.
- Displaying meaningful headings instead of field names, and adding other text when needed.
- Displaying data in forms other than one-line-per-record, across-the-page, accounting style. You can place data anywhere on the screen or printed page, as best suits the needs of the user.
- Trimming and changing data to be more readable. Field data with blank spaces can be trimmed. Coded data can be interpreted and meaningful words printed instead of terse codes.

Output can be sent to either a printer or screen. To keep these two media distinct, I shall use the verb *display* when referring to screen output and *print* for printer output. Like everything else in dBASE there are several ways to create output reports.

Using the dBASE Report Generator

dBASE has a report generator that is somewhat similar to the input screen generator. Use it to create simple "accounting style" reports. The report generator will ask you for a report heading, column headings, and footer information. You then specify the widths of columns and the fields to be placed in each column. You are limited to one record per line. Frankly, the report generator is difficult to use, especially if the data for each record cannot fit within one line.

IV The Report Writer in IV has been greatly improved but is complex. If you have IV, it may be worth taking the time to learn how to use it.

Using the Custom Input Screen for Output

You may use the input screens created in chapter 8 to display records. This is useful when you wish to edit displayed data. Used this way, the program usually searches for a record to be displayed. Then, the commands:

```
SET FORMAT TO <screen name>
READ
```

are used to display the record. There is no APPEND BLANK, but there still must be a READ.

The following command before the READ will print the input screen on a printer. GETs are ignored and SAYs are directed to the printer:

```
SET DEVICE TO PRINT
```

Be careful about using the input screen as a printed report if it has boxes, lines, and other graphics. Some printers cannot handle them; they may print as garbage. Some dot matrix or laser printers will print graphics if you first send a control code. The following code enables most Epson-compatible printers to print lines and boxes:

```
SET PRINT ON
? CHR(27) + CHR(116) + CHR(1)

HP Laserjet printers use the following: ? CHR(27) + '(10U'
```

Creating Output Reports With @...SAY and ?

I recommend this method for greatest flexibility although it requires a bit of planning, practice, trial, and error to get everything to display or print just right.

Chapter 8 described the use of @...SAY and ? to format input screens. The same techniques are used to format output screens. Recall that screen rows are numbered from 0 to 23 while columns are numbered from 0 to 79. Numbers larger than these cause errors. The hard part of creating spiffy reports is to decide where on the screen (or printout) everything should go and coming up with appropriate column and row parameters.

Printing @...SAYs

SAYs may be sent to a printer by first issuing the command:

```
SET DEVICE TO PRINT
```

All subsequent SAYs go to the printer *instead of* the screen. Notice that you must choose between screen or printer; you cannot use SAYs for both at the same time. If you wish to return to screen display, issue:

```
SET DEVICE TO SCREEN
```

There are some important differences between screen display and printing of SAYs:

- Unlike the screen limitation of 24 lines, paper is continuous. The row parameter can be up to 32,767. If you want neat pages with top and bottom margins, you must include a program routine for keeping track of the number of lines printed and then skipping to a new page when the page is full. The printer skips to the top of a new page with the command EJECT.
- If the printer receives a row value that is less then the previous value, it ejects to a new page. Unlike a screen, where you may display data anywhere, in any order, even from the bottom up, printers must be continuously moving down the page. Although many printers can reverse direction, dBASE III+ does not take good advantage of it.
- Most printers use a variety of print pitches, allowing a printed line length of more than 80 columns. The programmer must figure out the appropriate line length for the pitch (i.e., 80 columns for 10 pitch, 135 for compressed, etc.).
- PROW() and PCOL() are functions that return the printer head position. They are printer equivalents to ROW() and COL() for screens:

```
@ PROW(), PCOL() SAY <expn>
```

This prints <expn> where the print head last finished printing. A variation of this is useful when you wish to print on the same line and a few columns over. The following example prints the ISSN, skips 2 spaces and prints the copy number on the same line:

```
SET DEVICE TO PRINT
a 5, 10 SAY ISSN
a PROW(), PCOL() + 2 SAY COPY
```

Printing ?s

The question mark normally displays data on the screen but you may use it to send data to a printer. Use the command:

```
SET PRINT ON
```

to send subsequent ?s to *both* printer and screen. Notice that this differs from SET DEVICE TO PRINT which sends SAYs only to the printer. To disable the printer use:

```
SET PRINT OFF
```

Printing Underlines, Compressed, Other Characters

You may use ? CHR(xx) to control the printer for underlining words, using compressed print, italics, and printing graphic symbols. The number inside the parenthesis is a control code, and depends on the printer. You must consult the printer manual to find out what codes turn a feature on and off.

The following example shows how to underline a title (contained in TITLE) with an Epson-compatible printer:

```
SET PRINT ON
? CHR(27)+CHR(45)+CHR(1) + TITLE + CHR(27)+CHR(45)+CHR(0)
```

The sequence of codes before TITLE begins underlining, and the sequence following ends it. Here is how to do the same thing on a HP Laserjet printer:

```
? CHR(27)+CHR(38)+CHR(100)+CHR(68) + TITLE +;
CHR(27)+CHR(38)+CHR(100)+CHR(64)
```

Turn on compressed print on an Epson-compatible printer with ? CHR(15), and turn in off with ? CHR(18). On a Laserjet printer, use the following pair to turn compressed on and off:

```
? CHR(27)+CHR(38)+CHR(107)+CHR(50)+CHR(83)
? CHR(27)+CHR(38)+CHR(107)+CHR(48)+CHR(83)
```

The CHR() function may also be used to print special graphic symbols. Most of these use ASCII codes, but some printers must be sent a code in advance, setting it up for graphics. Some printers cannot print graphic characters at all. Consult your printer manual.

IV dBASE IV adds a STYLE option to ? for printing in various styles. Follow the expression to be printed with the word STYLE and one of the following letters:

```
B--bold
I--italic
U--underline
R--superscript
L--subscript
```

The following example will underline the title:

```
? TITLE STYLE "U"
```

Programs 11.1 and 11.2 illustrate some of these processes. The first example finds a title if the ISSN is unknown. An interesting feature of SRCH.PRG is that it finds titles if any part is known. It also permits you to store any of the ISSNs to use upon return to the calling program.

PROGRAM 11.1 SRCH.PRG Search for Titles

```
 1  *PROGRAM  SRCH.PRG
 2  *THIS PROGRAM ALLOWS A QUICK SEARCH BY TITLE
 3  *OR KEY WORD FROM THE TITLE
 4  *IT IS CALLED FROM MAINMENU.PRG, CHECKIN.PRG, FCHECK.PRG
 5  SET TALK OFF
 6  CLEAR
 7  @  1, 33  SAY "ANYTOWN LIBRARY"
 8  @  2, 29  SAY "SERIALS CONTROL SYSTEM"
 9  @  3, 36  SAY "TITLE SEARCH"
10  @ 4,1 TO 4,79 DOUBLE
11  USE BIB
12  MISSN = SPACE(9)
13  DO WHILE .T.
14     MTITLE = SPACE(30)
15     @ 5,0 CLEAR
16     @ 5,1 SAY 'Titles may be searched by typing any of the following:'
17     @ 7,5 SAY 'THE ENTIRE TITLE, including articles;'
```

```
18    @ 8,5 SAY 'THE FIRST FEW WORDS of the title;'
19    @ 9,5 SAY 'A SINGLE KEY WORD in the title.'
20    @ 10,5 SAY 'The more of the title which is typed in, the
         more accurate the retrieval.'
21    @ 12,1 SAY 'TYPE TITLE WORDS OR <RETURN> TO EXIT: ' GET
         MTITLE
22    READ
23    MTITLE = TRIM(MTITLE)
24    IF LEN(MTITLE) = 0
25      RETURN
26    ENDIF
27    LOCATE FOR UPPER(MTITLE) $ UPPER(TITLE)
28    @ 5,0 CLEAR
29    DO WHILE FOUND()
30      ? ISSN + "   " + TRIM(TITLE) + "   " + FREQ + "   " + PUBLISHER
31      ?
32      CONTINUE
33      IF ROW() > 20
34        WAIT
35        @ 5,0 CLEAR
36      ENDIF
37    ENDDO
38    WAIT
39    @ 21,1 SAY 'IF YOU WISH TO STORE AN ISSN, TYPE IT HERE';
40      GET MISSN
41    READ
42  ENDDO
```

NOTES ON SRCH.PRG

This program has three major sections:

1. Display heading and open BIB, lines 6-11.
2. Display instructions and GET the title, lines 12-23.
3. Display information about all serials that match the entered title words, lines 30-38.

Lines 22-28: Using $ to find any part of a title
This section asks the user for a word or words from the desired title:

```
@ 12, 1 SAY "TYPE TITLE WORDS OR <RETURN> TO EXIT: ' GET
MTITLE
READ
```

The $ in Line 28 is the "contains in" function. Used in conjunction with LOCATE, it searches through each record in the file to see if any part of TITLE matches the string of characters in MTITLE. Both MTITLE and TITLE must be in the same case; upper and lower cases of the same letters are not equivalent. The UPPER functions in Line 28 *temporarily* changes both MTITLE and TITLE to upper case for comparisons. The actual title is not changed on the file:

```
LOCATE FOR UPPER(MTITLE) $ UPPER(TITLE)
```

Unfortunately, you cannot use $ with SEEK, so this program uses LOCATE.

Lines 30-38: Display all candidate titles
Since the search may be ambiguous, it is important to display all titles that contain the characters in MTITLE. This loop uses the FOUND() function to display all titles that meet the LOCATE requirement:

```
DO WHILE FOUND()
   ? ISSN + "   " + TRIM(TITLE) + "    " + FREQ + "    " + PUB-
LISHER
   ?
   CONTINUE
   .
   .
ENDDO
```

Lines 34-37: Waiting when screen is full
If there are many titles matching the search string, you do not want them scrolling off the screen. This routine stops the display when the screen row becomes greater than 20. The program pauses and waits for the user to press any key (WAIT) and then clears the screen from row 5 and continues:

```
IF ROW() > 20
   WAIT
   a 5,0 CLEAR
ENDIF
```

PRINTING CLAIM NOTICES

Program 11.2 illustrates some complex print statements. It prints a list of journals that should be claimed (a more complex program would print actual claim notices).

PROGRAM 11.2 CLAIMSUM.PRG Print Summary of Claims

```
1  *PROGRAM CLAIMSUM.PRG
2  *TO GENERATE SUMMARY LIST OF
3  *PERIODICALS NEEDING TO BE CLAIMED
4  SET TALK OFF
5  USE MREC
6  COPY TO CLAIM FOR ACTION = "F" .OR. ACTION = "S"
7  USE CLAIM
8  APPEND FROM DREC.DBF FOR ACTION = "F" .OR. ACTION = "S"
9  APPEND FROM WREC.DBF FOR ACTION = "F" .OR. ACTION = "S"
10 SELECT 1
11 USE CLAIM
12 SELECT 2
13 USE COPY INDEX ISSNCOP
14 SELECT 3
15 USE BIB INDEX ISSNDEX
16 SELECT 1
17 SET DEVICE TO PRINT
18 SET PRINT ON
19 @  1, 33  SAY "ANYTOWN LIBRARY"
20 @  2, 29  SAY "SERIALS CONTROL SYSTEM"
21 @  4, 32 SAY "SUMMARY OF CLAIMS"
22 @  5, 1 SAY DATE()
23 ? CHR(15)
24 ? "ISSN     COPY     VENDOR     MISSING ISSUES       CLAIM #"
25 ?? "          TITLE                      PUBLISHER"
26 ? "                                VOL  ISSUE   DATE"
27 ? REPLICATE("-",135)
28 ?
29 LINECOUNT = 10
30 DO WHILE .NOT. EOF()
31    @ PROW(),1 SAY ISSN + "    " + STR(COPY,2)
32    SET RELATION TO ISSN + STR(COPY,2) INTO COPY
33    @ PROW(),PCOL()+9 SAY COPY->VEND_CODE + "         ";
34       + STR(VOL,4) + " " + STR(ISSUE,4) + "     " + DTOC(TOD)
35    @ PROW(),PCOL()+7 SAY ACTION
36    SET RELATION TO ISSN INTO BIB
37    @ PROW(),PCOL()+9 SAY BIB->TITLE + "   " + BIB->PUBLISHER
38    ?
39    LINECOUNT = LINECOUNT + 2
40    IF LINECOUNT > 60
41       EJECT
42       LINECOUNT = 0
```

```
43    ENDIF
44    SKIP
45  ENDDO
46  ? CHR(18)
47  SET PRINT OFF
48  SET DEVICE TO SCREEN
49  CLOSE DATABASES
50  ERASE CLAIM.DBF
51  RETURN
```

NOTES ON CLAIMSUM.PRG

This program has three major sections:

1. A way to combine data from several files, lines 5-16.
2. Print header and column headings, lines 19-28.
3. Print information from files, lines 30-45.

Lines 5-9: Relating Files
This program uses data from five files. It creates a new file called
CLAIMS.DBF that contains records from MREC, WREC, and DREC in
which the ACTION field contains an F or S. During printing, a relation
is set between this new file and BIB or COPY to print appropriate data
from those files.

Line 6 first copies records from MREC to CLAIM. This makes a new,
temporary file. Lines 8 and 9 append records from DREC and WREC to it:

```
USE MREC
COPY TO CLAIM FOR ACTION = "F" .OR. ACTION = "S"
USE CLAIM
APPEND FROM DREC.DBF FOR ACTION = "F" .OR. ACTION = "S"
APPEND FROM WREC.DBF FOR ACTION = "F" .OR. ACTION = "S"
```

Line 23, 46: Printer Control Codes
? CHR(15), sends an ASCII 15 to the printer. This code turns most dot
matrix printers to compressed print of 16 or 17 pitch with about 135
columns across the page. ? CHR(18), returns the printer to normal pitch.

Lines 31-37: PROW() and PCOL()
PROW() and PCOL() are used to control the print position of data:

```
DO WHILE .NOT. EOF()
   a PROW(), 1 SAY ISSN + "   " + STR(COPY,2)
   SET RELATION TO ISSN + STR(COPY,2) INTO COPY
```

```
@ PROW(), PCOL()+9 SAY COPY->VEND_CODE + "        ";
  + STR(VOL,4) + " " + STR(ISSUE,4) + "     " + DTOC(TOD)
@ PROW(), PCOL+7 SAY ACTION
  .
  .
```

Line 32, 36: Setting Relationships
These lines set relationships first between CLAIM and COPY based on
the common ISSN/COPY combination:

```
SET RELATION TO ISSN + STR(COPY,2) INTO COPY
```

and then between CLAIM and BIB to print title and publisher:

```
SET RELATION TO ISSN INTO BIB
```

DELETING RECORDS

In the course of events, it becomes necessary to erase or delete
unwanted records from one or more databases. Deletions become necessary when a serial is no longer purchased by the library and there is
no need to keep old check-in data. Sometimes the record is placed in an
archive file before being deleted.

If the library drops an entire serial, you will probably want to delete
everything, including check-in data. If only one copy is dropped, you will
probably drop the appropriate copy and its check-in data but leave other
copies intact.

A section of the program should first find and display the doomed
record to make sure it is the right one. It is unwise to delete records
without confirmation.

Deleting a record requires two commands: DELETE which only
marks a record for deletion, and PACK which actually deletes it. You
can delete several records before packing, but one PACK wipes out all
outstanding DELETEs. The usual method is to locate the record (using
LOCATE or SEEK), display it and ask for verification, then delete and
pack it.

As long as a database file has not been packed, records which have
been deleted can be restored, listed, moved to another database, and so
on. You may reinstate any record that has been marked for deletion, *but
not yet packed*, by issuing the command:

```
RECALL
```

DELETE and RECALL have several similar options. I will concentrate on DELETE. Some examples are shown below:

```
DELETE 4 (marks record #4 for deletion)
DELETE NEXT 5 (marks the next 5 records for deletion)
DELETE ALL (be careful with this one)
DELETE FOR ISSN = MISSN
DELETE WHILE ISSN = MISSN
DELETE FOR PUBLISHER = "Bad News Publishing Co."
```

Remember that FOR operates on all records meeting the condition and WHILE quits when it finds the first record not meeting the condition. The fourth example marks for deletion *all* records in which the ISSN equals the data stored in MISSN. The next example marks for deletion only those which match until the first non-matching record is reached. If the record pointer is already on a record which does not match, no records are deleted.

There are two ways to wipe out *all* records in a file but still retain the empty file. They are rarely used except in program development, and should be used with care. One way is:

```
DELETE ALL
PACK
```

and the other is:

```
ZAP
```

(no PACK needed).

Program 11.3 deletes entire serials or single copies. It is complex because there are 5 data files involved, each with an index, and verification and caution are built into each step.

PROGRAM 11.3 SERDEL.PRG Delete Serials

```
 1  *PROGRAM: SERDEL.PRG
 2  *THIS PROGRAM DELETE RECORDS.
 3  SET TALK OFF
 4  SELECT 1
 5  USE BIB INDEX ISSNDEX
 6  SELECT 2
 7  USE COPY INDEX ISSNCOP
 8  SELECT 1
 9  MISSN = SPACE(9)
10  DO WHILE .T.
```

```
11    CLEAR
12    @  1, 33  SAY "ANYTOWN LIBRARY"
13    @  2, 29  SAY "SERIALS CONTROL SYSTEM"
14    @  3, 36 SAY "DELETION"
15    @ 4,1 TO 4,79 DOUBLE
16    MCOPY = 1
17    @ 5,1 SAY 'Enter ISSN' GET MISSN
18    @ 6,1 SAY "Enter <RETURN> to Exit"
19    READ
20    IF LEN(TRIM(MISSN)) = 0
21      CLOSE DATABASES
22      RETURN
23    ENDIF
24    SEEK MISSN
25    IF EOF()
26      @ 21,1 SAY 'THAT PERIODICAL NOT FOUND'
27      @ 22,1 SAY 'ENTER ANOTHER ISSN OR <RETURN>'
28      WAIT
29      LOOP
30    ENDIF
31    DEL = 3
32    @ 5,0 CLEAR
33    @ 5,0 SAY 'ISSN: ' +ISSN
34    @ 5,17 SAY 'Frequency: '+FREQ
35    @ 6,0 SAY 'Title: '+TITLE
36    @ 7,0 SAY 'Publisher: '+PUBLISHER
37    @ 10,2 SAY "Do you wish to:"
38    @ 12,4 SAY "1 = DELETE this ENTIRE periodical, including
39      all check-in records"
40    @ 13,4 SAY "2 = DELETE only one copy of this periodical"
41    @ 14,4 SAY "3 = Do NOT delete anything." GET DEL PICTURE "9"
42    READ
43    DO CASE
44      CASE DEL = 3
45        LOOP
46      CASE DEL = 1
47        OK = " "
48        DO WHILE .NOT. OK $ "YyNn"
49          ACCEPT "Are you sure Y/N? " TO OK
50        ENDDO
51        IF UPPER(OK) = "N"
52          SELECT 1
53          LOOP
54        ENDIF
```

```
55   ENDCASE
56   DO CASE
57     CASE FREQ = "D"
58       SELECT 3
59       USE DREC INDEX DREC
60     CASE FREQ = "W" .OR. FREQ = "BW"
61       SELECT 3
62       USE WREC INDEX WREC
63     OTHERWISE
64       SELECT 3
65       USE MREC INDEX MREC
66   ENDCASE
67   DO CASE
68     CASE DEL = 1
69       SELECT 1
70       DELETE
71       PACK
72       SELECT 2
73       DELETE FOR ISSN = MISSN
74       PACK
75       SELECT 3
76       DELETE FOR ISSN = MISSN
77       PACK
78     CASE DEL = 2
79       SELECT 2
80       MCOPY = 1
81     @ 15, 4 SAY "Copy number to delete: " GET MCOPY PICTURE "99"
82       READ
83       SEEK MISSN + STR(MCOPY,2)
84       DELETE
85       PACK
86       SELECT 3
87       DELETE FOR COPY = MCOPY
88       PACK
89     ENDCASE
90     SELECT 1
91   ENDDO
```

NOTES ON SERDEL.PRG

Let us look at major sections of this program. Most of the commands have been covered before. It would be instructive for the reader to go through this program and examine:

- DELETE options used
- use of SELECT to move from file to file
- use of CASE statements to make decisions.

1. Open files and initialize variables, lines 4-9.
2. Display header, ask for ISSN, search BIB, lines 11-24.
3. Display record, asks user for decision, uses DO CASE to act on the decision, lines 32-55.
4. Open appropriate check-in file, lines 56-66.
5. Delete record(s), lines 67-89.

Lines 32-41, 48-50: Serial Verification

Before deleting, it is important to display enough of the record to allow the user to identify it. First, the user is given choices to delete the entire periodical, one copy only, or go back to choose another ISSN or quit, in case it is the wrong periodical. If the user chooses the last option, the program loops to Line 10:

```
DEL = 3
@ 5, 0 CLEAR
@ 5, 0 SAY 'ISSN: ' +ISSN
.
@ 10, 2 SAY "Do you wish to:"
@ 12, 4 SAY "1 = DELETE this ENTIRE periodical, including
all check-in records"
@ 13, 4 SAY "2 = DELETE only one copy of this periodical"
@ 14, 4 SAY "3 = Do NOT delete anything." GET DEL PICTURE
"9"
READ
```

If the choice is made to delete the entire serial, Lines 48-50 ask if the user is sure. It uses the $ function to permit a response of Y or N only:

```
DO WHILE .NOT. OK $ "YyNn"
   ACCEPT "Are you sure Y/N? " TO OK
ENDDO
```

Lines 56-66: Choosing the Check-in Data File

The next DO CASE selects DREC, WREC, or MREC, depending on the frequency of the serial. Only one database file is SELECTed (remember, only *one* set of CASE statements is executed; the rest are ignored). Later in the program, SELECT 3 will activate the proper file:

```
DO CASE
CASE FREQ = "D"
       SELECT 3
       USE DREC INDEX DREC
CASE FREQ = "W" .OR. FREQ = "BW"
       SELECT 3
       USE WREC INDEX WREC
OTHERWISE
       SELECT 3
       USE MREC INDEX MREC
ENDCASE
```

Lines 67-89: Deleting

The next DO CASE finally deletes the records. If the user chooses to delete the entire serial (DEL = 1), BIB is selected and the record deleted. Next, it deletes all records from COPY with that ISSN (Lines 72-74). Finally, it selects the proper check-in file and deletes records from it (Lines 75-77):

```
DO CASE
CASE DEL = 1
       SELECT 1
       DELETE
       PACK
       SELECT 2
       DELETE FOR ISSN = MISSN
       PACK
       SELECT 3
       DELETE FOR ISSN = MISSN
       PACK
```

If the user chooses to delete only a copy, the program jumps to Line 78 where it selects COPY. Line 81 asks for the copy to delete. The program searches the index for the ISSN/COPY and deletes the record. Finally, it deletes the records from the appropriate check-in file:

```
CASE DEL = 2
  SELECT 2
  MCOPY = 1
  a 15, 4 SAY "Copy number to delete: " GET MCOPY PICTURE
"99"
  READ
  SEEK MISSN + STR(MCOPY,2)
  DELETE
```

```
    PACK
    SELECT 3
    DELETE FOR COPY = MCOPY
    PACK
ENDCASE
```

Deleting records is a necessary, but potentially dangerous database activity. The programmer should build in safeguards before finally deleting data. At least, the candidate record should be displayed and the user asked to verify the decision to delete ("Are you sure?").

12

Putting It All Together

We have examined separately some processing activities that make up a dBASE serials control system. But a system is not a system until components interact; until it all hangs together. Here are some ways to pull programs and databases together into a working whole.

MODULAR PROGRAMMING

The idea of programming a complex, multi-functional, multi-database system seems overwhelming at first. Like most of life's challenges, it becomes manageable when taken one small task at a time. Break down the task into several modules, each of which accomplishes a specific function. A circulation control system would have separate modules to add records to the database, charge out books, discharge books, place holds, send overdue notices, and so on. Short programs that do specific things are easier to write and test. Problems are confined to fewer lines of code and it is easier to keep track of what is going on. They can be debugged without involving the whole system.

Inexperienced system designers sometimes develop menus as the first step. This is definitely getting the cart before the horse. Design functional modules first. Then, as the system develops, begin thinking of menus and other devices for pulling it all together.

There are three kinds of program modules:

Control programs
These are programs that act to initialize a system, serve as bridges between programs, set up environmental conditions, or call other programs. The most common type in this category is the menu.

MAINMENU.PRG (Program 12.1) is the main control program for the Serials System. It is the first, last, and intermediate interface between the system and the user. The user begins with this menu, is taken back to it between operations, and quits from there. Although it is important, it should not be developed first. I shall discuss menus more fully later.

Although not a menu, CHECKIN.PRG (Program 8.2), is another type of control program. Its job is to choose which of several subprograms to use during the check-in process. It makes the choice automatically on the basis of data in the record.

Functional programs
These are developed around a single function, like adding or deleting serials, listing serials due to expire, searching for titles, printing claimnotices, and so on. They are the most common type of program module.

Routines
These are utility programs that do repetitive tasks throughout the system. Examples might be routines for displaying repeated messages and prompts on the screen, calculating overdue charges or withholding taxes, breaking long lines to fit neatly on a screen or printout,[1] and so on. Experienced programmers keep a library of routines to modify as needed.

dBASE SUBPROGRAMS

Modular programming is possible because dBASE programs can call other programs. The process is quite simple. Unlike other languages, there is no difference between programs and subprograms (except for one special case to be described later). A program might be a subprogram in one activity and a main program in another, and the only real distinction is in which one "calls" which. "Calling" means to load another program into memory and turn control over to it. I sometimes refer to programs as *calling programs* and subprograms as *called programs*.

The following command calls another program:

```
DO <program name>
```

The called program is then executed until it hits a RETURN statement, whereupon control returns to the statement immediately following the DO in the calling program. Figure 12.1 illustrates this:

FIGURE 12.1 Subprogram Flow

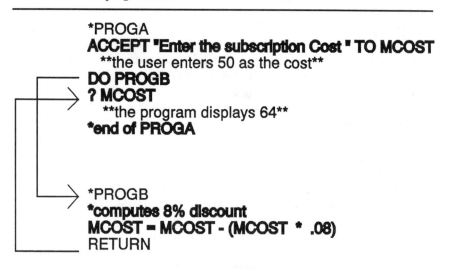

Subprograms may be nested to any depth. Any called program may call another program, which in turn may call another, and so on. Each called program needs a RETURN to get back to its calling program. There is one important caution: *never have a called program call a calling program; always use RETURN to "walk" back.*

Moving Data Between Programs

What happens to data in memory as you move from program to subprogram? Can data generated by one program be used by others? Sometimes.

Notice in Figure 12.1 that PROGA contains the following statements:

```
ACCEPT "Enter the subscription cost: " TO MCOST
DO PROGB
```

When PROGB is called what happens to the data in MCOST? Nothing. It is still there and available for PROGB or any subprogram. PROGB may change MCOST and the change can be used by PROGA. Suppose, in Figure 12.1, the user enters 50 as the subscription cost. The program jumps to PROGB and computes the 8% discount. When it returns to PROGA, the statement ? MCOST will display 46. This is because of the following rule concerning data sharing: *Variables created by a calling program may be used and changed by any called program.*

This does not work if the called program creates the variable. Consider these changes in Figure 12.1:

```
*PROGA.PRG
ACCEPT "Enter the subscription cost: " TO MCOST
**the user enters 50 as the cost**
DO PROGB
? TOTCOST
**the program displays "Variable not Found"**
*END OF PROGA

*PROGB.PRG
*COMPUTES 8% DISCOUNT
TOTCOST = MCOST - (MCOST * .08)
RETURN
```

Upon RETURN from PROGB, TOTCOST is lost. This is because of another rule: *variables created by called programs cannot be used by calling programs.* In other words, called programs may use and change data first created by calling programs but calling programs may not use data first created by called programs.

There is a way around this. By adding the following command in PROGA, a variable created in any subprogram is available to all programs. You may list any number of variables after the word PUBLIC:

```
PUBLIC TOTCOST
```

Data Exchange Using Parameters

Another, more explicit way to exchange data among subprograms is to send them through parameters. Notice the changes in these programs:

```
*PROGA.PRG
ACCEPT "Enter the subscription cost: " TO MCOST
**the user enters 50 as the cost**
DO PROGB WITH MCOST, TOTCOST
? TOTCOST
**the program displays 46**
*END OF PROGA

*PROGB.PRG
*COMPUTES 8% DISCOUNT
PARAMETERS MCOST, TOTCOST
```

```
TOTCOST = MCOST - (MCOST * .08)
RETURN
```

The important things here are the DO...WITH... in the calling program, and PARAMETERS... in the subprogram. The calling program "sends" the cost through MCOST and "receives" the computed total through TOTCOST. The subprogram picks up the cost in MCOST, calculates the discount, and sends the results back through TOTCOST.

It is not necessary for the variable names to be the same. One program could have used A and B instead of MCOST and TOTCOST. dBASE matches the variables in the DO WITH and those in PARAMETERS by position, not by name. The PARAMETERS statement must be the first non-comment line in the subprogram.

PROCEDURE FILES

When your system is nearly complete, tested, and debugged, and assuming you do not compile it, you may wish to make a procedure file. This is a single file of some or all programs and subprograms. Use a word processor that saves documents as ASCII text and combine all the .PRGs into one file. They do not have to be in any particular order.

Add the following statement as the first line of each program and subprogram:

```
PROCEDURE <program name>
```

No other changes are necessary except each program must have a RETURN (which they should have anyway). Give the procedure file a name—let's call it DOIT.PRG.

Below is a very simple example of three programs combined into a procedure file called DOIT. Asterisks (which are a good idea, but not required) separate the programs.

```
*PROCEDURE FILE DO IT
PROCEDURE PROGA
INPUT "Enter the subscription cost: " TO MCOST
DO PROGB
DO PROGC
QUIT
****
PROCEDURE PROGB
MCOST = MCOST - (MCOST * .08) && computes 8% discount
RETURN
```

```
****
PROCEDURE PROGC
? MCOST
RETURN
```

PROGA accepts the subscription cost, PROGB calculates the discount, and PROGC displays the results. You would never use three separate programs for such a simple task (this is modular programming taken to extremes!); I included them here only for illustration.

To activate the procedure, place the following statements in a program that is *not* part of DOIT (a main menu program is a good place):

```
SET PROCEDURE TO DOIT
DO PROGA
CLOSE PROCEDURE
```

The last statement, not surprisingly, closes the procedure and releases it from memory. SET PROCEDURE TO <another file> also closes the current one.

The advantage of procedure files is that the system operates faster with far less disk access. As separate programs, each must be loaded into memory when called, and as often as called. Procedure files are loaded only once. Calls to the individual procedures (programs) are almost instantaneous. You can call any of the procedures as often as needed, and in any order.

It is not necessary to include every program in a procedure file. Those which remain outside the procedure will be called in the normal way even if a procedure is active. If dBASE cannot find the called program in the procedure file, it goes to the disk in the normal fashion. You may have more than one procedure file, although only one may be active at a time.

dBASE III allows a maximum of 32 programs in each procedure file. dBASE IV has a theoretical limit of 1,170, although RAM size will most likely limit the number.

MENUS

The challenge of modular programming is to pull all the programs, subprograms, and routines together into a system. The workhorse of program integration is the menu. Remember that a menu is nothing but another program, usually the first one called.

Well designed, well integrated menus help the user make efficient use of a complex system. Poorly designed menus, or a hodgepodge of poorly integrated, multiple menus can be disastrous.

One philosophy of menu construction says to use a single menu from which all functional programs are chosen. All activities start and end with one menu. The Serials System uses this approach as the main menu calls all ten serials control functions. There are no submenus, although some functional programs ask for additional choices. Figure 12.2(a) is a diagram of the single menu organization used by the Serials System.

FIGURE 12.2   Menu Organizations

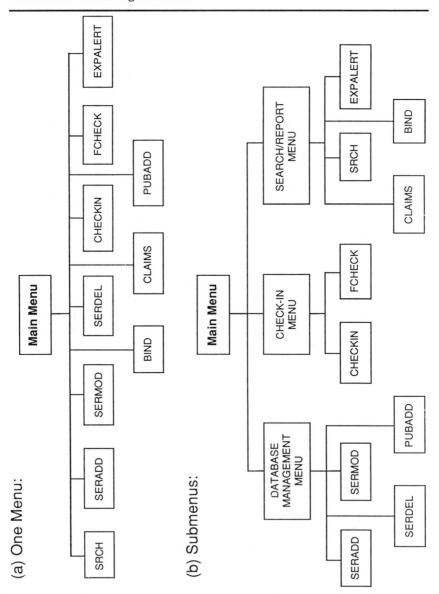

An alternative is like decentralized management. It groups related functions under submenus. A main menu calls submenu programs, which may call yet other submenus, and so on. Finally, you reach a functional program. For example, Figure 12.2(b) shows how you might group the programs under; database management; check-in, and search/report, each with its own menu.

Each approach has advantages and disadvantages. It gets tiresome having to navigate a complex series of submenus, wending your way back and forth through various strata of menus. This is especially painful if the most frequently used functions are several strata down. On the other hand, a series of well developed submenus gives a logical structure to the system, allowing users to work on related activities in groups.

Choices for Menu Options

Menu choices may be numbers, letters, or mnemonics. Figure 12.3 shows examples of each. Which you use is a matter of style. Number choices are a bit easier to program. It is best not to mix them, although some designers advocate alternating numbers and letters in successive submenus. Mnemonics should be inherently meaningful.

The examples in Figure 12.3 are simple. Other, more complex menu types are moving bar, pop-up, and pull-down. You can program these in dBASE III+ but only with difficulty, and the results are not always satisfactory.[2]

IV dBASE IV added several programming commands to create pull-down, pop-up, and bar menus. They allow you to use overlapping windows, colors, and graphics. It is still a complex programming task requiring study and experimentation.[3]

Navigating Menus

Whether or not you use submenus, it is my belief that everything should begin and end with menus. It should not be possible to quit the system from a functional program. When a function is finished, the user should have the option of returning to the main menu (perhaps to choose another function), quitting from a submenu (if you use submenus), or returning to the previous menu.

All programs, subprograms, menus, and submenus should have a RETURN as the last logical statement (whether it is the last physical statement depends on the logical structure of the program). This command returns to the most immediate calling program. If the calling program is a menu or submenu, return will be to it.

FIGURE 12.3   Menu Choices

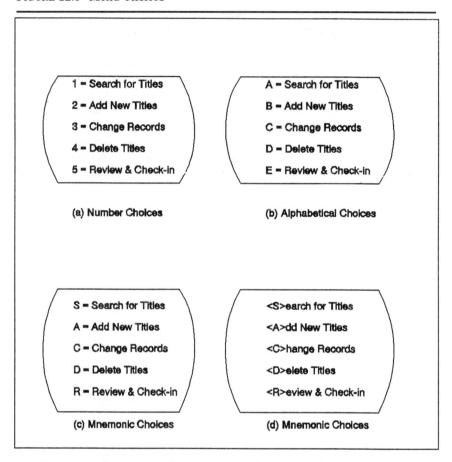

To return from any subprogram to the first calling program (most likely the main menu), use:

```
RETURN TO MASTER
```

All subprograms should use RETURN or RETURN TO MASTER to get back to MAINMENU; none of them should contain the statement: DO MAINMENU. In fact, never have a called program call any calling program.   dBASE will let you do it, but each time that command is invoked, dBASE loads additional copies of MAINMENU into memory, and then additional copies of functional programs. Repeated use of DO MAINMENU will put several copies of all your programs in memory simultaneously. You will soon get a message that says: "Too many files open."

Opening and Closing Database Files in Menus

A complex menu system poses the question of when to open and close database files. If you have only one or two files, it may be best to open them all at the beginning of the main menu and close them all just before quitting the system. This way, they are available for use by all programs.

If your system uses many files or a complex set of menus, it may be best to open only those needed in each functional module and close them before leaving the module. This avoids having too many files open simultaneously. Also, so long as a file is open it is susceptible to damage; it is safer to keep files open no longer than necessary.

On the other hand, continually closing and reopening files slows the system. If you use the same file in several modules, it may be best to open and close it once from the main menu.

SERIALS SYSTEM MAIN MENU

The Serials System main menu (PROGRAM 12.1) is simple but gets the job done. It is a single menu, calling most other programs from it.

```
1   * PROGRAM: MAINMENU.PRG
2   * THIS IS THE CONTROL MODULE FOR ALL PROGRAMS IN THE
3   * SERIALS CONTROL CHECK-IN SYSTEM
4   SET TALK OFF
5   IF YEAR(DATE()) < 1985
6      CLEAR
7      ? "IT IS ESSENTIAL THAT TODAY'S DATE BE ENTERED "
8      ? "DURING BOOT-UP.  PLEASE ENTER DATE"
9      RUN DATE
10  ENDIF
11  DO WHILE .T.
12     CLEAR
13     ? "   " + CMONTH(DATE()) + " " + STR(DAY(DATE()),2);
14       + ", " + STR(YEAR(DATE()),4)
15     @ 2, 12 SAY "A N Y T O W N   S E R I A L S   C H E C K - I N"
16     @ 4, 30 SAY "M A I N   M E N U"
17     @ 6, 6 SAY "1 = SEARCH FOR TITLES        6 = FAST CHECK-IN"
18     @ 8, 6 SAY "2 = ADD NEW TITLES OR COPIES        7 =  BINDERY
                                              INFORMATION"
19     @ 10,6 SAY "3 = CHANGE BIBLIOGRAPHIC RECORDS    8 =
                                              EXPIRATION ALERT"
20     @ 12,6 SAY "4 = DELETE TITLES        9 = CLAIM NOTICES"
21     @ 14,6 SAY "5 = REVIEW & CHECK-IN    10 = PUBLISHER INFO "
```

```
22    @ 3,1 to 15,79 DOUBLE
23    CHOICE = "  "
24    @ 17, 3 SAY "Choose a number or type Q to QUIT: " GET CHOICE
25    READ
26    SET EXACT ON
27    DO CASE
28     CASE UPPER(CHOICE) = "Q"
29        RETURN
30     CASE (CHOICE) = "1"
31        DO SRCH
32     CASE CHOICE = "2"
33        DO SERADD
34     CASE CHOICE = "3"
35        DO SERMOD
36     CASE CHOICE = "4"
37        DO SERDEL
38     CASE CHOICE = "5"
39        DO CHECKIN
40     CASE CHOICE = "6"
41        DO FCHECK
42     CASE CHOICE = "7"
43        DO BIND
44     CASE CHOICE = "8"
45        DO EXPALERT
46     CASE CHOICE = "9"
47        DO CLAIMS
48    CASE CHOICE = "10"
49        DO PUBADD
50     ENDCASE
51    ENDDO
```

NOTES ABOUT MAINMENU.PRG

This program has three major parts:

1. Check to make sure the computer has stored today's date, lines 5-10.
2. Display menu and ask for choice, lines 11-25.
3. Call subprogram, depending on the choice, lines 27-50.

Lines 5-10: Make sure date is entered
The Serials System requires that you enter today's date when booting the computer. The function YEAR(DATE()) returns the year of today's

date. If the year is less than 1985, RUN (Line 9) executes the DOS DATE command which prompts the user for a date:

```
IF YEAR(DATE()) < 1985
   CLEAR
   ? "IT IS ESSENTIAL THAT TODAY'S DATE BE ENTERED "
   ? "DURING BOOT-UP.  PLEASE ENTER DATE"
   RUN DATE
ENDIF
```

Lines 13-14: Displaying the Date
This complex statement displays the date in the form: August 16, 1990. Each part of this statement derives a portion of the date: month name, day, and full year. These are combined with commas and spaces. The easier alternative, ? DATE(), would display it as 08/16/90:

```
? "   " + CMONTH(DATE()) + " " + STR(DAY(DATE()),2);
+ ", " + STR(YEAR(DATE()),4)
```

Line 26: SET EXACT ON
This command assures that comparisons in the CASE statements be exact. dBASE would normally compare what is in CHOICE with the *first character* in the CASE conditions, confusing "10" with "1".

Lines 27-50: Calling Appropriate Subprogram
Most of the cases in this DO CASE call subprograms (e.g., DO SRCH). When the program returns from a subprogram, execution continues with Lines 50, 51, and 11, in that order:

```
DO CASE
     CASE UPPER(CHOICE) = "Q"
          RETURN
     CASE (CHOICE) = "1"
          DO SRCH
     .
     .
ENDCASE
```

AUTOMATIC ACTIVATION OF PROGRAMS

Starting a program is easy once you get into dBASE. Just type DO MAINMENU (or whatever is the name of the first program) at the dot prompt. However, the goal is to make the system stand-alone as much as possible. Ideally, the main menu should be the first thing the user sees. He or she should make choices from it and not have to worry about getting into dBASE or typing DO anything.

There are several ways to activate the main menu automatically. The best way is to compile the programs into .EXE programs and get away from dBASE altogether. I recommend compiling for serious applications (compilers are discussed below).

Besides compiling, there are two other ways to activate your system with little operator intervention. The first way is to include the first program name in the DOS command line:

```
C> DBASE MAINMENU
```

This assumes that you have set the correct path and that MAIN MENU is in the same directory as dBASE. A DOS menu program will even eliminate this step (two good ones are AUTOMENU, Magee Enterprises, Norcross, GA, and Take Charge!, DTI, Newton, NJ). The operator just chooses SERIALS SYSTEM from the menu.

If this method does not appeal to you, another way is to have dBASE call the first program. To do this, you must have, or modify, a file called CONFIG.DB and make sure it is in the directory that contains dBASE (you may use a word processor, EDLIN, or MODI COMM to create or modify it).

CONFIG.DB may contain any number of dBASE "start-up" commands such as setting the default drive (DEFAULT = A), whether to have the status bar at the bottom of the screen or not (STATUS = OFF), how may decimals to display (DECIMALS = 2), and so on. The important thing for us is to add the following line to it:

```
COMMAND = DO MAINMENU
```

This line must be the last (or only) line in CONFIG.DB. It starts MAINMENU after you displaying dBASE's license agreement screen. There is no way to avoid the license screen, short of compiling programs.

COMPILING dBASE PROGRAMS

Compiling is the best way to make a stand-alone, working system. A compiled program becomes an .EXE file the same as most of the software you purchase (in fact, some purchased software starts out as dBASE programs). The compiled program runs from DOS without the necessity of first loading (or even buying) dBASE.

dBASE III+ is an interpreted language. The interpreter translates instruction into machine language each time the program runs. This slows program execution. It also requires that the user have dBASE on the computer to run programs.

Compilers create machine language files that run faster and do not need dBASE when running. dBASE IV partially compiles programs for faster execution, but they still cannot stand alone without further compilation.

Since compilers are separate packages, I will not try to describe how to use them here; they all work differently. Compiled programs may be distributed and run without requiring the use of either dBASE or the compiler.

Following are a few dBASE III compilers. These not only compile dBASE III+ programs but they also add their own enhancements to the original language:

- Clipper, Nantucket Corp., Los Angeles, Calif
- FoxBase Plus, Fox Software, Perrysburg, Ohio.
- Quicksilver, Wordtech Systems, Orinda, Calif.

VALIDITY CHECKS AND ERROR TRAPPING

I wish to conclude this chapter with a discussion of one of the most important topics in systems design. A guiding slogan of computer programming is: "If a user can make a mistake, he will." Validity checks insure that entered data are correct or fall within acceptable ranges. Error traps are ways in which you anticipate some of the things which might go wrong—some of the mistakes a user might make—and either prevent them from happening or take necessary corrective action.

It is impossible to trap for all errors, but it is foolish not to trap for as many as you can anticipate. Incredibly, many expensive, commercial programs are inadequate in error trapping. Their developers go on the false assumption that people read and follow directions. They falsely believe every user is as familiar with the program as the developers. Good program development requires "cold," naive users to test the program before release. This is "beta testing."

Types of Errors

Errors can generally be classified as preventable, correctable, recoverable, fatal, and device-related.

- Preventable errors are those that you can prevent from happening altogether. dBASE has some built-in functions to do this and I will show a few examples later.

- Correctable errors are those in which incorrect data can be corrected through the editing process, or by taking a series of planned steps to remedy problems.
- Recoverable errors are those which cause the program to halt temporarily and wait for a corrective response. Or they might send the user back to a menu to start over. Good error trapping keeps recoverable errors from becoming fatal ones.
- Fatal errors are those which cause the program either to hang up (freeze) or "bomb." When a program freezes, the best analogy is that it is confused. The program does not know what to do—it hangs in an infinite loop or gets lost in some ROM routine. Freezing may be the fault of the program or the user. Sometimes fatal errors happen when you run programs on computers and peripherals for which they were not designed. A program bombs when it suddenly goes back to DOS. Imagine that you are using a data entry program when suddenly the program stops and you are back to the DOS prompt. At the bottom of the screen is C>. Your data entry program is no longer working. You may be able to recover eventually, but data entry is halted and some data may be lost. In the worst case, a disk will be wiped out.
- Device errors may be fatal but they are usually neither the fault of the programmer or user. They happens when the program tries to read from or write to a flawed or damaged disk. A simple, and recoverable, error of this type is "Drive not ready error." This usually means that the disk drive door is open. Sometimes it signals faulty hardware. A more serious error, "Read fault," means the operating system cannot read data from the disk. Most likely, it is caused by a damaged disk, but it also may suggest a hardware problem.

dBASE Error Messages

When dBASE encounters an error, it halts execution of the program and displays a message that describes the error. This is followed by a question: "Cancel, Ignore, Suspend? (C, I, or S)." The programmer should trap errors so that the user never sees this message. If it does happen, the user must decide which of the three options to choose and what to do next.

- Cancel stops program execution, closes all files, and sends you back to the dot prompt. Sometimes you can fix the problem and start over. Sometimes data and disks are seriously damaged.
- Ignore tries to ignore the statement(s) that caused the error and skips over them. Sometimes this works, sometimes it does not, and sometimes the results are worse than canceling.

- Suspend temporarily stops execution of the program and returns to the dot prompt. If the user knows how, he or she may type commands at the dot prompt to correct the problem, or find out what is causing it. The program continues by typing RESUME.

PROGRAMMING ERROR TRAPS

I now turn to specific functions and routines to evaluate user data input and trap for errors. It is not possible to trap for every conceivable, or inconceivable, error. The routines suggested in this section trap for the most common ones so the user is not faced with the choices described in the above paragraph.

Preventing Errors

Good programs minimize the possibility of fatal errors, but no program can anticipate every mistake. The way to catch unanticipated errors is to place the following command as one of the first lines:

```
ON ERROR <do something>
```

The <do something> part can be any dBASE command. Usually it is a DO <subprogram>, as in the following example, where it calls ERRPROG.PRG. What should ERRPROG do? The programmer must work out a suitable course of action for each program. As a minimum, the subprogram should CLOSE DATABASES and RETURN TO MASTER:

```
ON ERROR DO ERRPROG
```

Preventing Escape

If the user accidentally hits **Esc** while entering data, the results may be catastrophic. There are two ways to avoid or minimize the effects of hitting the Esc key. One or other of the following commands (but not both) may be placed at the beginning of a program:

```
SET ESCAPE OFF
ON ESCAPE  <do something>
```

The first command causes **Esc** to be ignored. The second causes some planned action if it is pressed. The planned action may beany dBASE command or a subprogram.

"Must-Fill" Fields

These are fields that must have data in them before you can move on. A must-fill field in the Serials System is the ISSN, since everything else depends on it.

dBASE does not have an automatic must-fill function although dBASE IV's VALID option to @...GET comes close. The following program fragment illustrates one way of making sure the ISSN has data:

```
DO WHILE .T.
  MISSN = SPACE(9)
  a 5, 1 SAY "Enter ISSN, or Q to quit: " GET MISSN
  READ
  IF LEN(TRIM(MISSN)) = 0
     ? "You must enter an ISSN"
     ? "Please go back to enter ISSN"
     WAIT
     LOOP
  ENDIF
  .
  .
ENDDO
```

Duplicate Data

Sometimes data, like the ISSN, must be unique from record to record. The following fragment checks the file to make sure the ISSN has not already been used:

```
DO WHILE .T.
  MISSN = SPACE(9)
  a 5,1 SAY "Enter ISSN, or Q to quit: " GET MISSN
  READ
  SEEK MISSN
  IF .NOT. EOF()
     ? "That ISSN already on file"
     ? "Please enter another ISSN"
     WAIT
     LOOP
  ENDIF
  .
  .
ENDDO
```

Correct Data Type

As we know, dBASE uses "pictures" to make sure entered data are of the correct type. Pictures prevent the user from entering characters when numbers are expected. A program with the following command will not move on until the user enters two numeric digits:

```
a 6,1 SAY "Enter Copy Number" GET MCOPY PICTURE "99"
```

Range Checks

For numeric data, you may wish to make sure that data fall within a specified range. A RANGE statement is added to the GET. The following example makes sure the user enters a number from 1 to 25.

```
a 6, 1 SAY "Enter Copy Number" GET MCOPY PICTURE "99"
RANGE 1,25
```

Date variables or fields do not use pictures or ranges; they contain built-in checks. You must always enter a valid date into a field or variable designated as DATE type; it will not accept 02/31/88, for example.

Correct Coded Choices

The serials copy data use a series of codes to represent vendors (F, D, M, O). The program should check to make sure the user entered a valid code. There are several ways to do this.

One way uses the "contained in" function ($). In the following, read the DO WHILE statement as: "Stay in the loop as long as the contents of MVEND are not contained in the string 'FDMO'." If the user types anything other than those letters, it keeps asking:

```
MVEND = " "
  DO WHILE .NOT. MVEND $ "FDMO"
  a 7,1 SAY "Enter Vendor Code: " GET MVEND
  READ
ENDDO
```

This routine can be used effectively for yes/no questions, such as "Is this correct?," "Do you wish to continue?," "Do you wish to delete this serial?":

```
OK = " "
DO WHILE .NOT. OK $ "YyNn"
```

```
    ACCEPT "Is this correct Y/N?" TO OK
ENDDO
```

Another way to ensure correct coded choices is to use coded phrase files[4] or "picklists"[5] which display, and sometimes force use of, only the correct choices.

Correct Menu Choices

What happens if the user accidentally types a response that is not among the choices in a menu? The DO CASE structure has a built in check. If a choice is not in the CASE statements, it "falls through" to the next statement after ENDCASE. If the next statement is the end of a loop, the program jumps back to redisplay the menu. You also may use an OTHERWISE to catch incorrect menu choices.

Reasonable Data

This is the most difficult to predict and plan for. It checks to see if entered data are reasonable. For example, an annual subscription cost of $0 might be reasonable but $.50 might not. Or a library might subscribe to ten copies of one journal, but probably not to 100 copies.

One way is to use a series of IF statements. An easier way is to ask the user to verify critical data:

```
OK = "N"
DO WHILE UPPER(OK) = "N"
  ACCEPT "Enter Cost: " TO MCOST
  ACCEPT "Is this correct? Y/N " TO OK
ENDDO
```

This stays in the loop, continually asking for cost, until the user responds to the question with Y.

There are two problems with this approach. One is that you cannot verify every bit of entered data; reserve this for very critical data that will make a difference later. The second problem is that there is no way to incorporate loops and IFs within screens made with dBASE III+ screen painting utility. You must write your own screen formatting programs to include these kinds of checks.

Checking Status of Equipment

The most common error trap in this category is to make sure the printer is turned on. If the printer is off when SET PRINT ON is issued, the system responds with "Printer not connected. Cancel, Ignore, Suspend?" Although the user can take corrective action, it makes for some uncomfortable moments and opens possibilities for user mistakes.

A better solution is to precede SET PRINT ON with a warning. Although this does not actually check the status of the printer, it waits until the user physically checks and presses a key:

```
WAIT "Press any key when printer is ready . . . "
SET PRINT ON
```

IV dBASE IV has a useful function, PRINTSTATUS (), that returns TRUE if the printer is ready. It can be used as follows:

```
IF .NOT. PRINTSTATUS ()
   WAIT "Turn printer on and press any key"
ENDIF
```

Endnotes

1. This, and many other useful routines are described in Alan Simpson. *Advanced Techniques in dBASE III Plus*. (San Francisco: Sybex, 1986).
2. For programming techniques, see: Alan Simpson. *Advanced Techniques in dBASE III Plus*. (San Francisco: Sybex, 1986).
3. Good sources of information on creating dBASE IV menus are: *Using dBASE IV* (Carmel, Ind.: Que Corporation, 1990); Edward Jones. *dBASE IV Programmer's Reference Guide* (Indianapolis: Howard W. Sams & Co., 1989).
4. Yerkey, A. Neil, "Using Coded Phrase Databases in dBASE", *Microcomputers for Information Management* 1989 6(3):207:218.
5. Edward Jones. *dBASE IV Programmer's Reference Guide* (Indianapolis: Howard W. Sams & Co., 1989).

13

Other Library Examples

We have followed the development of a Serials Control System through the steps of database design, screen design, indexing, searching, and reporting. I hope this progression has shown the activities necessary to get from data to information, and that you have learned some of the ins and outs of dBASE programming along the way.

The introduction listed several library applications that can benefit from microcomputer information management using a database management system. The principles and techniques described so far can be applied to most of these. To solidify the ideas, I wish now to examine a few other library applications. All programs listed in this chapter are "bare bones," and some are only representative modules from larger systems. In actual use they need to be dressed up with headings, instructions to users, more error traps, additional functions, and various bells and whistles. Previous chapters have explained most of the commands used in these programs, so this chapter will not contain extensive notes about them.

AN INVENTORY CONTROL SYSTEM

This is an example of using dBASE to manage a single database—a flat file. It is designed to store and display data about library equipment scattered around a building or system. The data elements are typical, but the fields could easily be modified for other situations. This example also illustrates how to use a procedure file.

The system is built around an "Asset Number." This is a unique accession number assigned to all new equipment. Although not an absolute requirement in a flat file, it is always a good idea to have some unique identifier for each record.

The example programs give a listing of equipment by asset number and by description. The listing by description allows the user to type any part of the description. Other listings not shown, but easily added, might be by P.O. number and room/building/area location. Another enhancement would be to add routines to total the cost of equipment on the listings.

The database is called INV.DBF and is indexed on ASSETNO to ASSET.NDX. Figure 13.1 shows its structure.

FIGURE 13.1   INV.DBF Structure

```
Structure for database: B:inv.dbf

Field   Field Name   Type        Width     Dec    Comments

    1   DATEIN       Date           8              Date in file

    2   PONO         Character      6              P.O. No

    3   BLDG         Character     11              Building

    4   ROOM         Character      5

    5   ASSETNO      Character     10              Asset No

    6   DESC         Character     30              Description

    7   FL           Numeric        3       0      Floor

    8   MANUFAC      Character     20              Manufacturer

    9   MODEL        Character     10

   10   S            Character      1              Status

   11   FUND         Character      1              Acct Fund

   12   C            Character      1              Condition

   13   SERIAL       Character     20              Serial No

   14   COST         Numeric        8       2

   15   ACDT         Date           8              Date Rcvd

   16   COMMENT      Character     75

** Total **                       218
```

The main menu is called INVMENU.PRG (PROGRAM 13.1). It generates the screen shown in Figure 13.2.

```
*INVMENU.PRG
*MAIN MENU PROGRAM
SET TALK OFF
SET BELL OFF
SET STATUS OFF
SET CONFIRM ON
PUBLIC LINECT
USE INV INDEX ASSET
SET PROCEDURE TO INVPRO
DO WHILE .T.
   CLEAR
   CHOICE = 0
   @ 2,29  SAY "ANYTOWN PUBLIC LIBRARY"
   @ 3,28  SAY "PROPERTY CONTROL SYSTEM"
   @ 4,5 SAY DATE()
   @ 4,35  SAY "MAIN MENU"
   @ 7,5   SAY "1 = Add New Equipment            4 = List
                                 Equipment By Asset No"
   @ 9,5   SAY "2 = View or Change Equipment    5 = List
                                 Equipment by Description"
   @ 11,5 SAY "3 = Delete Equipment"
   @ 13,5 SAY "0 = QUIT"
   @ 17,5 SAY "Enter Choice ==>" GET CHOICE PICTURE '#'
   @ 1,2  TO 18,78 DOUBLE
   @ 5,3  TO  5,77
   READ
   DO CASE
      CASE CHOICE = 0
         SET PROCEDURE TO
         CLOSE DATABASES
         RETURN
      CASE CHOICE = 1
         DO INVADD
      CASE CHOICE = 2
         DO INVCHANG
      CASE CHOICE = 3
         DO INVDEL
      CASE CHOICE = 4
         DO INVASSET
      CASE CHOICE = 5
```

```
      DO INVDES
   ENDCASE
   END DO
```

FIGURE 13.2 Inventory System Menu

```
                        ANYTOWN PUBLIC LIBRARY
                        PROPERTY CONTROL SYSTEM
    01/25/91                  MAIN MENU
    
    1 = Add New Equipment          4 = List Equipment By Asset No
    
    2 = View or Change Equipment   5 = List Equipment by Description
    
    3 = Delete Equipment
    
    0 = QUIT
    
    
    Enter Choice ==> 0
```

The menu starts a procedure file called INVPRO.PRG (Program 13.2) that contains all programs necessary to run the inventory system:

```
INVPRO.PRG PROCEDURE FILE FOR INVENTORY
*CONTROL SYSTEM
****
PROCEDURE INVADD
*PROGRAM TO ADD, CHANGE, OR DISPLAY EQUIPMENT
DO WHILE .T.
   CORRECT = 'C'
   APPEND BLANK
   DO WHILE UPPER(CORRECT) = 'C'
      CLEAR
      DO INVSCRN
      READ
      CORRECT = ' '
      DO WHILE .NOT. UPPER(CORRECT) $ 'ACQ'
         @ 21, 20 say "Hit C to change; A to add more; Q to quit"
GET CORRECT
         READ
      ENDDO
   ENDDO
   REPLACE DATEIN WITH DATE()
   IF UPPER(CORRECT) = 'Q'
   DELETE FOR LEN(TRIM(ASSETNO)) = 0
      PACK
```

```
      RETURN
    ENDIF
  ENDDO
  *****
  PROCEDURE INVCHANG
  *PROGRAM TO CHANGE INVENTORY RECORDS
  DO WHILE .T.
    CLEAR
    @ 1,2 SAY DATE()
    @ 1,29  SAY "ANYTOWN PUBLIC LIBRARY"
    @ 2,27  SAY "PROPERTY CONTROL SYSTEM"
    MASS = SPACE(10)
    @ 3,2 TO 7,79
    @ 4,5 SAY "Enter Asset Number of Equipment to Change or
    View"
    @ 5,5 SAY "Or Press Enter to Quit ==>" GET MASS
    READ
    IF LEN(TRIM(MASS)) = 0
      RETURN
    ENDIF
    SEEK MASS
    IF EOF()
      ANY = ' '
      @ 4,5 CLEAR TO 5,75
      @ 4,5 SAY "That Asset Number not found--Try again    "
      @ 5,5 SAY "Press any key to continue...."  GET ANY
      READ
      @ 4,5 CLEAR TO 5,75
      LOOP
    ENDIF
    CORRECT = 'C'
    CLEAR
    DO WHILE UPPER(CORRECT) = 'C'
      DO INVSCRN
      READ
      CORRECT = ' '
      DO WHILE .NOT. UPPER(CORRECT) $ 'ACQ'
          @ 21, 20 say "Hit C to change; A for another; Q to quit"
GET CORRECT
          READ
      ENDDO
    ENDDO
    IF UPPER(CORRECT) = 'Q'
      RETURN
```

```
    ENDIF
ENDDO
****
PROCEDURE INVDEL
*PROGRAM TO DELETE INVENTORY RECORDS
SET INDEX TO ASSET, PO
DO WHILE .T.
  CLEAR
  a 1,2 SAY DATE()
  a 1,29  SAY "ANYTOWN PUBLIC LIBRARY"
  a 2,27  SAY "PROPERTY CONTROL SYSTEM"
  MASS = SPACE(10)
  a 3,2 TO 7,79
  a 4,5 SAY "Enter Asset Number of Equipment to Delete"
  a 5,5 SAY "Or Press Enter to Quit ==>" GET MASS
  READ
  IF LEN(TRIM(MASS)) = 0
    RETURN
  ENDIF
  SEEK MASS
  IF EOF()
    ANY = ' '
    a 4,5 CLEAR TO 5,75
    a 4,5 SAY "That Asset Number not found--Try again    "
    a 5,5 SAY "Press any key to continue...."  GET ANY
    READ
    a 4,5 CLEAR TO 5,75
    LOOP
  ENDIF
  CLEAR
  DO INVSCRN
  CLEAR GETS
  CORRECT = ' '
  DO WHILE .NOT. UPPER(CORRECT) $ 'YN'
    a 21,23 SAY "Is this the record to delete Y/N?" GET CORRECT
    READ
  ENDDO
  IF UPPER(CORRECT) = 'Y'
    DELETE
    PACK
  ENDIF
ENDDO
****
PROCEDURE INVSCRN
```

```
*SCREEN GENERATION ROUTINE
@ 5,55 SAY DATE()
@ 3,3 SAY "Building:" GET BLDG
@ 3,47 SAY 'ANYTOWN PUBLIC LIBRARY'
@ 4,3 SAY "Room No.:" GET ROOM
@ 4,47 SAY "PROPERTY CONTROL SYSTEM"
@ 5,6 SAY "Floor:" GET FL
@ 8,2 SAY "PO Number:" GET PONO
@ 8,20  SAY "Asset Number:" GET ASSETNO
@ 10,2 SAY "Description:" GET DESC
@ 10,46 SAY "Status:" GET S PICTURE '!'
@ 10,56 SAY "Condition:" GET C PICTURE '!'
@ 11,46 SAY "Fund Code:" GET FUND PICTURE '!'
@ 12,2  SAY "Manufacturer:" GET MANUFAC
@ 12,38  SAY "Model:" GET MODEL
@ 12,56  SAY "Ser:" GET SERIAL FUNCTION "S15"
@ 14,2  SAY "Cost:" GET COST
@ 14,18  SAY "Acquisition date (mm/dd/yy):" GET ACDT
@ 16,2 SAY "Comments:" GET COMMENT FUNCTION "S60"
@ 20,24  SAY "Exit anytime by pressing Ctrl End"
@ 19,19 to 22,63
@ 1,0  TO  17,79 DOUBLE
@ 6,2  TO  6,78
RETURN
****
PROCEDURE INVASSET.PRG
*PROGRAM TO LIST BY ASSET NUMBER
POS = 'S'
CLEAR
@ 5, 5 SAY "Do you wish to list on the SCREEN (S) or
PRINTER (P)?"
@ 6,5 GET POS PICTURE '!'
READ
PR = IIF(POS = 'P',.T.,.F.)
IF PR
   WAIT 'Make sure printer is ready and press any key to con-
tinue...'
   SET PRINT ON
   SET MARGIN TO 10
ENDIF
GO TOP
CLEAR
? SPACE(22) + " ANYTOWN PUBLIC LIBRARY"
? SPACE(22)+ "LISTING BY ASSET NUMBER"
```

```
    ? 'REPORT AS OF ' + DTOC(DATE())
    ? REPLICATE('_',69)
    LINECT = 5
    DO WHILE .NOT. EOF()
      MASSET = ASSETNO
      DO WHILE ASSETNO = MASSET
        DO DISPIT
        SKIP
      ENDDO
    ENDDO
    ****
    PROCEDURE INVDES
    *PROGRAM TO LIST BY DESCRIPTION
    POS = 'S'
    CLEAR
    @ 5, 5 SAY "Do you wish to list on the SCREEN (S) or
PRINTER (P)?"
    @ 6,5 GET POS PICTURE '!'
    READ
    PR = IIF(POS = 'P',.T.,.F.)
    IF PR
      WAIT 'Make sure printer is ready and press any key to con-
tinue...'
      SET PRINT ON
      SET MARGIN TO 10
    ENDIF
    GO TOP
    CLEAR
    ? SPACE(22) + "ANYTOWN PUBLIC LIBRARY"
    ? SPACE(22)+  "LISTING BY DESCRIPTION"
    ? 'REPORT AS OF ' + DTOC(DATE())
    ? REPLICATE('_',69)
    LINECT = 5
    DO WHILE .T.
      @ 8,0 CLEAR
      MDESC = SPACE(20)
      @ 9,5 SAY 'Type in as much of the description as you know.'
      @ 11,5 SAY 'Use the singular form. For example: printer,
terminal,
    computer.'
      @ 12,5 SAY 'The description can be in upper or lower case,
and can be'
      @ 13,5 SAY 'any part of the description (computer
retrieves
```

```
     microcomputer).'
        @ 14,5 SAY 'TYPE DESCRIPTION OR <RETURN> TO EXIT: ' GET
MDESC
     READ
     MDESC = UPPER(TRIM(MDESC))
     IF LEN(MDESC) = 0
       RETURN
     ENDIF
     GO TOP
     LOCATE FOR MDESC $ UPPER(DESC)
     @ 6,0 CLEAR
     IF .NOT. FOUND()
       ? 'No records found with that description.'
       WAIT 'Press any key to type another description or quit...'
       LOOP
     ENDIF
     ? 'DESCRIPTION: ' + MDESC
     ? REPLICATE('.',69)
     DO WHILE FOUND()
       DO DISPIT
       CONTINUE
     ENDDO
     IF PR
       ?
       EJECT
       SET PRINT OFF
     ENDIF
     WAIT
   ENDDO
   ****
   PROCEDURE DISPIT
   *PROGRAM TO PRINT OR DISPLAY RECORDS
   ?'Building:       ' + BLDG
   ?'Room:           ' + ROOM
   ?'Floor:          ' + STR(FL,2)
   ?"PO Number:      " + PONO
   ?"Asset Number:   " + ASSETNO
   ?"Description:    " + DESC
   ?"Status: " + S + "   Condition: " + C + "   Fund Code: " +
FUND
   ?"Manufacturer:   " + MANUFAC
   ?"Model:          " + MODEL
   ?"Ser:            " + SERIAL
   ?"Cost:          $" + STR(COST,8,2)
```

```
?"Acquisition date: " + DTOC(ACDT)
?"Comments:          " + LEFT(COMMENT,60)
? REPLICATE('.',69)
LINECT = LINECT + 15
IF PR
  IF LINECT > 50
    EJECT
  ENDIF
ELSE
  WAIT 'Press SPACE to continue; Q to quit' TO QUITIT
  IF UPPER(QUITIT) = 'Q'
    RETURN TO MASTER
  ENDIF
  CLEAR
ENDIF
```

Procedures in INVPRO add records (PROCEDURE INVADD), view or change records (PROCEDURE INVCHANG), and delete records (PROCEDURE INVDEL). These three programs make use of a screen generation procedure called INVSCRN. Figure 13.3 shows a sample screen:

FIGURE 13.3 Inventory System Input Screen

```
┌──────────────────────────────────────────────────────────────────┐
│                                                                    │
│   Building:                       ANYTOWN PUBLIC LIBRARY           │
│   Room No.:                       PROPERTY CONTROL SYSTEM          │
│     Floor:                             01/25/91                    │
│  ───────────────────────────────────────────────────────────────  │
│  PO Number:      Asset Number:                                     │
│                                                                    │
│  Description:                          Status:   Condition:        │
│                                        Fund Code:                  │
│  Manufacturer:                 Model:           Ser:               │
│                                                                    │
│  Cost:          Acquisition date (mm/dd/yy):   /  /                │
│                                                                    │
│  Comments:                                                         │
│                                                                    │
└──────────────────────────────────────────────────────────────────┘

        ┌──────────────────────────────────────────────┐
        │      Exit anytime by pressing Ctrl End        │
        └──────────────────────────────────────────────┘
```

There are two procedures to display data. One listing is by asset number (PROCEDURE INVASSET) and one is by description (PROCEDURE INVDES). Both ask if you want to display the listings on a screen or printer, and they make use of an output generation procedure called DISPIT.

REFERENCE BOOKS SUBJECT SEARCH

This simple example is a database of reference books. It might be used by new reference staff to help them identify possible reference sources in response to subject inquiries. I have presented it here to illustrate two things:

- how to add records to two database files
- how to conduct a simple subject search.

It uses two database files. The main file is BOOK.DBF, a bibliographic file that is indexed on ISBN to ISBNDEX.NDX. The structure is shown in Figure 13.4:

FIGURE 13.4   BOOK.DBF Structure

```
Structure for database:  B:book.dbf

Field   Field Name   Type        Width     Dec

    1   ISBN         Character      12

    2   CALLNO       Character      15

    3   AUTHOR       Character      20

    4   TITLE        Character      30

    5   PUBLISHER    Character      30

    6   DATE         Numeric         4       0

** Total **                       112
```

The second file is SUBJECT.DBF. It contains only two fields: ISBN and SUBJECT. For each record in BOOK, there may be several records in SUBJECT, each containing one subject keyword for each reference source.

Only two modules are shown here: a program to add records to the database, and one to search by subject. A complete system would need modules to change records, delete records, and do other types of searches. It would be pulled together with a main menu, also not shown.

Program 13.3, BOOKADD.PRG, adds records to the two files. It uses a customized screen to add records to BOOK.DBF, and then selects SUBJECT.DBF to allow the user to add as many subjects as necessary. The ISBN is automatically added to the subject records.

PROGRAM 13.3   BOOKADD.PRG Reference Books Input

```
*BOOKADD.PRG
*PROGRAM TO INPUT DATA INTO TWO DATABASES
SET TALK OFF
SELECT 1
USE BOOK INDEX ISBNDEX
SELECT 2
USE SUBJECT
MOREBOOKS = 'Y'
*INPUT INTO BOOKS.DBF
DO WHILE UPPER(MOREBOOKS) = 'Y'
   SELECT 1
   SET FORMAT TO BOOKS
   APPEND BLANK
   READ
   MISBN = ISBN
   SET FORMAT TO
   MORESUBS = 'Y'
   SELECT 2
   *INPUT INTO SUBJECT.DBF
   DO WHILE UPPER(MORESUBS) = 'Y'
      SET CARRY ON
      APPEND BLANK
      REPLACE ISBN WITH MISBN
      MSUB = SPACE(10)
      @ 12,1 SAY ISBN
      @ 13,1 SAY "Enter subject for this reference book."
      @ 14,1 SAY "Leave blank if no more subjects: " GET SUBJECT
      READ
      *NO MORE SUBJECTS IF LEFT BLANK
      IF LEN(TRIM(SUBJECT)) = 0
         DELETE
         PACK
         MORESUBS = 'N'
      ENDIF
   ENDDO
   SET CARRY OFF
   @ 21,0 CLEAR
   ACCEPT 'Type Y to add another book; Q  to quit' TO
MOREBOOKS
ENDDO
CLOSE DATABASES
RETURN
*END OF PROGRAM
```

Program 13.4, BOOKSRCH.PRG, searches SUBJECT.DBF for desired subjects. It uses the LOCATE command, so partial subject wording will work. If it finds a subject entry, it stores the ISBN and then selects, searches, and displays the record from BOOK.DBF. It then asks if the user wishes to see other books on the subject, or go back and search for another subject.

PROGRAM 13.4 BOOKSRCH.PRG Reference Books Search

```
*BOOKSRCH.PRG
*PROGRAM TO SEARCH DATABASE BY SUBJECT
SET TALK OFF
SET BELL OFF
SELECT 1
USE BOOK INDEX ISBNDEX
SELECT 2
USE SUBJECT
DO WHILE .T.
   CLEAR
   MSUB = SPACE(10)
   a 5,5 SAY "Type the desired subject keyword; hit Enter to
quit:";
       GET MSUB
   READ
   IF LEN(TRIM(MSUB)) = 0
     CLOSE DATABASES
     RETURN
   ENDIF
   *SEARCH SUBJECT.DBF FOR KEYWORD
   LOCATE FOR UPPER(SUBJECT) = UPPER(MSUB)
   DO WHILE FOUND()
     MISBN = ISBN
     SELECT 1
     *SEARCH BOOK.DBF FOR FOUND ISBN
     SEEK MISBN
     CLEAR
     a 2,5 SAY "SUBJECT--" + TRIM(MSUB) + ":"
     a 3,5 SAY "ISBN: " + ISBN
     a 4,2 SAY "CALL NO: " + CALLNO
     a 5,3 SAY "AUTHOR: " + AUTHOR
     a 6,4 SAY "TITLE: " + TITLE
     a 7,0 SAY "PUBLISHER: " + PUBLISHER
     a 8,5 SAY "DATE:"
     a 8,12 SAY DATE
```

```
      SELECT 2
      CON = ' '
      @ 19,1 SAY "Do you wish to see other books under this sub-
ject Y/N?" GET CON
      READ
      IF UPPER(CON) # 'Y'
        EXIT
      ENDIF
      CONTINUE
      IF .NOT. FOUND()
        @ 20,1 SAY "No more books listed under " + MSUB
        WAIT
      ENDIF
    ENDDO
  ENDDO
```

BOOLEAN SEARCHING OF DBASE FILES

dBASE is not well suited for sophisticated bibliographic search programs, in the style of Dialog or BRS. In the first place, its fixed field structure does not lend itself to bibliographic data. Secondly, the language is not designed for complicated Boolean searches. However, simple searches are possible, and I wish to illustrate some techniques using the reference book database.

Program 13.4 searched on one field for one subject. Searching on only one field is easy. I used the LOCATE command, but if the file had been indexed, I could have used SEEK. The complications come in when you want to use Boolean AND or OR on more than one field, or to use OR on a single field.

Boolean AND

Searching on two *different* fields with .AND. or .OR. is not difficult. Suppose, for example, you wanted to search BOOK.DBF on two fields, say AUTHOR and YEAR. Your search program would need lines similar to the following:

```
ACCEPT "Enter Author to search: " TO MAUTH
ACCEPT "Enter Year to search: " TO MYEAR
LOCATE FOR AUTHOR = MAUTH .AND. YEAR = MYEAR
```

Boolean OR on One Field

Searching two subjects using OR is a bit more complicated, but not difficult. Change Program 13.4 to include the following lines immediately after DO WHILE .T.:

```
DO WHILE .T.
CLEAR
   MSUB1 = SPACE(10)
   MSUB2 = SPACE(10)
   @ 5, 5 SAY "Type the first subject keyword; hit Enter to
quit:";   GET MSUB1
   @ 6, 5 SAY "Type the second subject keyword; hit Enter for
only one keyword:" GET MSUB2
   READ
   IF LEN(TRIM(MSUB1)) = 0
     CLOSE DATABASES
     RETURN
   ENDIF
   *
```

*The following IF routine is necessary in case the user enters only one keyword:

```
   *
   IF LEN(TRIM(MSUB2)) = 0
     LOCATE FOR SUBJECT = MSUB1
   ELSE
     LOCATE FOR SUBJECT = MSUB1 .OR. SUBJECT = MSUB2
   ENDIF
   .
   .
```

The most serious problem with the above examples is deciding how to provide these choices in programs: which fields to search, whether to OR or AND them, and so on. The user interface becomes more complicated than the search techniques.

Boolean AND on One Field

Searching on *one field* with .AND. is theoretically impossible! dBASE's .AND. requires comparison of *two fields*. Well, there has to be a way to do a Boolean AND on a single field. There is. What you have to do is to search the database for one subject (e.g., horses) and store the set of ISBN's that satisfy it in a temporary file. Then search for the *other* subject (e.g., pigs) and compare each ISBN found with the temporary stored set. Common ISBN's represent AND (horses AND pigs), and will be retrieved from the main file. See Program 13.5.

PROGRAM 13.5 BOOKLAND.PRG Boolean and Search

```
*BOOLAND.PRG
*THIS PROGRAM DOES A BOOLEAN AND SEARCH ON SUBJECTS
```

```
SET SAFETY OFF
SET TALK OFF
DO WHILE .T.
  ACCEPT 'Enter first subject term ' TO SUBJ1
  ACCEPT 'Enter second subject term ' TO SUBJ2
  TWOSUB = .F.
*THE FOLLOWING ROUTINE CREATES THE FILE HITS AND INDEXES IT
*ON ISBN. IT IS ONLY CREATED IF TWO SUBJECTS ARE REQUESTED.
  IF LEN(SUBJ2) > 0
    TWOSUB = .T.
    USE SUBJECT
*THE FOLLOWING STATEMENT CREATES HITS.DBF WHICH CONTAINS
ONLY
*THE ISBN'S FOR SUBJ2
    COPY TO HITS FIELDS ISBN FOR SUBJECT = SUBJ2
    USE HITS
    INDEX ON ISBN TO HITDEX
  ENDIF
*NOW THAT THERE IS A FILE OF ISBN'S WITH SUBJ2, OPEN EVERY-
THING
*AND CONTINUE
  SELECT 1
  USE SUBJECT
  SELECT 2
  USE BOOK INDEX ISBNDEX
  SELECT 3
  USE HITS INDEX HITDEX
  SELECT SUBJECT
  LOCATE FOR SUBJECT = SUBJ1
  DO WHILE FOUND()
    MISBN = ISBN
    IF TWOSUB    &&IF THERE ARE TWO SUBJECTS
      SELECT HITS
      SEEK MISBN
      IF EOF()
        ? 'NOTHING (MORE) FOUND'
        EXIT
      ENDIF
      SELECT BOOK
      SEEK MISBN
      ? AUTHOR
      ? TITLE
      ? SUBJ1
      ? SUBJ2
```

```
      ELSE          &&IF THERE IS ONLY ONE SUBJECT
        SELECT BOOK
        SEEK MISBN
        ? AUTHOR
        ? TITLE
        ? SUBJECT->SUBJECT
      ENDIF
      SELECT SUBJECT
      CONTINUE
    ENDDO
    CLOSE DATABASES
    ACCEPT 'Do you wish to search another subject Y/N? ' TO
NOTHER
    IF UPPER(NOTHER) = 'N'
      SET SAFETY ON
      RETURN
    ENDIF
  ENDDO
  *END OF PROGRAM
```

This program creates a temporary file (HITS.DBF) of the hits from one of the requested subjects. It then compares hits from the other subject against it. If there are any matches, the record from the main file will be displayed.

CIRCULATION CONTROL

The last two programs demonstrate two functional modules from a circulation control system. The first module uses a batch process to print overdue notices, and the second discharges books. Of course, a complete system would require a menu program, plus additional programs to maintain the database, inquire, place holds, and charge out books.

There are only two files in this demonstration set. BOOKOUT.DBF is the file of books charged out. This could be the main file for those systems that keep a file of only books on loan ("absence system"), or it could be derived from tagged records for those that maintain the full catalog ("inventory system"), or it could be a temporary transaction file. Besides some bibliographic data, it contains the charge-out date, the borrower number, and the loan type. The loan type is a single-letter code (T, N, M, P) representing 3 day, 14 day, 31 day, and permanent loan. It also has a field (NOTICENO) for recording how many notices have been sent. Figure 13.5 shows its structure:

FIGURE 13.5   BOOKOUT.DBF Structure

```
Structure for database: B:bookout.dbf

Field   Field Name   Type        Width    Dec    Comments

   1    BOOKNO       Numeric       6        0     Acc No

   2    AUTHOR       Character    25

   3    TITLE        Character    30

   4    DATEOUT      Date          8              Charge out

   5    TYPE         Character     1              Loan type

   6    BORROWNO     Numeric       6              Borrower No

   7    NOTICENO     Numeric       2              Notices sent

** Total **                      79
```

The other file, BORROWS.DBF, is a name and address file of all library patrons. It includes a record for all card holders whether or not they have books charged out. It contains the usual name/address data and its structure is shown in Figure 13.6:

FIGURE 13.6   BORROWS.DBF Structure

```
Structure for database: B:borrows.dbf

Field   Field Name   Type        Width    Dec    Comments

   1    BORROWNO     Numeric       6        0     Borrow No

   2    LASTNAME     Character    25

   3    FIRSTNAME    Character    20

   4    STREET       Character    45

   5    CITY         Character    25

   6    STATE        Character     2

   7    ZIP          Numeric       5        0

   8    TELEPHONE    Character    12

   9    MALE         Logical       1              Male?

** Total **                     142
```

The field labelled MALE should be explained. It is a logical field that really asks a question: "Is this patron a MALE?" At the risk of seeming to be sexist, everyone in the database is either male or not, and a Y or N goes into this field. It will be used in the overdue notice program to print the salutation, "Mr." or "Ms." This is a bit easier than having a SEX field with M or F in it. The field could be labelled FEMALE with a slight change in the program.

Program 13.6 prints an overdue letter. Notice that it uses the SET RELATION command to tie the BORROWERNO of the two files together.

PROGRAM 13.6 OVERDUE.PRG Circulation System Overdue Notices

```
*OVERDUE.PRG
*PROGRAM TO SEND OVERDUE NOTICES
SET TALK OFF
SELECT 1
USE BOOKOUT
SELECT 2
USE BORROWS INDEX BORROWS
SELECT 1
SET RELATION TO BORROWNO INTO BORROWS
SET PRINT ON
SET MARGIN TO 10
DO WHILE .NOT. EOF()
  DO CASE
    CASE TYPE = 'T'
      PERIOD = 3
    CASE TYPE = 'N'
      PERIOD = 14
    CASE TYPE = 'M'
      PERIOD = 31
    CASE TYPE = 'P'
      PERIOD = 365
  ENDCASE
  MDATEOUT = DATEOUT
  MDAYS = DATE() - MDATEOUT
  FINEDAYS = MDAYS - PERIOD
  IF FINEDAYS > 0
    SELECT 2
    SALUT = IIF(MALE, 'Mr.','Ms.')
    EJECT
    ? SALUT + ' ' + TRIM(FIRSTNAME) + ' ' + LASTNAME
    ? STREET
```

```
      ? TRIM(CITY) + ', '+ STATE + '  ' + STR(ZIP)
      ?
      ? 'Dear ' + SALUT + ' ' + TRIM(LASTNAME) + ':'
      ?
      ? '      ' + 'Our records show that the following book is
now '
      ?? STR(FINEDAYS,3)
      ?? ' days overdue.'
      ? 'Please return the book as soon as possible'
      ?? ' so that others may use it.'
      ? 'Thank you.'
      SELECT 1
      ?
      ? '  Book number: ' + STR(BOOKNO)
      ? '        Author: ' + AUTHOR
      ? '         Title: ' + TITLE
      ? 'Date borrowed: ' + DTOC(DATEOUT)
      REPLACE NOTICENO WITH NOTICENO + 1
      ? 'This is overdue notice ' + STR(NOTICENO,2)
   ENDIF
   SKIP
ENDDO
CLOSE DATABASES
RETURN
```

The program goes through the entire BOOKOUT file. The CASE statements and several statements following determine if the book is overdue. If so, the program prints the letter using data from both files and increments the NOTICENO field by one. Once started, there is no further user interaction.

The next program discharges a book, based on input of the book number. It only deletes records from BOOKOUT.DBF, leaving the borrower file intact.

PROGRAM 13.7 CHAROUT.PRG Circulation System Discharge

```
*CHAROUT.PRG
*PROGRAM TO DISCHARGE BOOKS
SET TALK OFF
SELECT 1
USE BOOKOUT
SELECT 2
USE BORROWS INDEX BORROWS
SELECT 1
SET RELATION TO BORROWNO INTO BORROWS
```

```
CLEAR
? SPACE(29) + 'ANYTOWN PUBLIC LIBRARY'
? SPACE(30) + 'CIRCULATION CONTROL'
? SPACE(32) + 'DISCHARGE MODULE'
? REPLICATE('-',79)
?
DO WHILE .T.
  MBOOKNO = 0
  @ 6,0 CLEAR
  @ 8,0 SAY 'Enter Book Number of book to discharge--Hit
                          Enter to quit' GET MBOOKNO
  READ
  IF MBOOKNO = 0
    CLOSE DATABASES
    RETURN
  ENDIF
  LOCATE FOR BOOKNO = MBOOKNO
  IF .NOT. FOUND()
    @ 10, 0 SAY 'No book in charge out file by that number'
    WAIT
    LOOP
  ENDIF
  @ 10,0 SAY AUTHOR
  @ 12,0 SAY TITLE
  @ 14,0 SAY 'Borrower:'
  @ 14,10 SAY BORROWS->BORROWNO
  @ 14,18 SAY BORROWS->LASTNAME
  ACCEPT 'Is this the book? Y/N ' TO ISIT
  IF UPPER(ISIT) = 'N'
    LOOP
    ENDIF
  DO CASE
    CASE TYPE = 'T'
      PERIOD = 3
    CASE TYPE = 'N'
      PERIOD = 14
    CASE TYPE = 'M'
      PERIOD = 31
    CASE TYPE = 'P'
      PERIOD = 365
  ENDCASE
  MDATEOUT = DATEOUT
  MDAYS = DATE() - MDATEOUT
  FINEDAYS = MDAYS - PERIOD
```

```
      FINE = FINEDAYS * .10
      IF FINE > 0
        ? 'There is a fine of ' + STR(FINE,5,2) + ' on this book.'
      ENDIF
      ACCEPT 'Discharge? Y/N ' TO KILLIT
      IF UPPER(KILLIT) = 'N'
        LOOP
      ELSE
        DELETE
        PACK
      ENDIF
   ENDDO
```

If you enter a book number of 0, the program quits. Otherwise, it searches BOOKOUT.DBF and displays some information from both files to verify if this is the one and to verify whether to discharge it. If the user answers no to either of these questions, it loops back to ask for another book number. Otherwise, it deletes the record from BOOKOUT. It uses the same routine as Program 13.6 to determine whether the book is overdue and also calculates and displays the fine.

Bibliography

This selected bibliography lists a few of the many books on information management which the reader may find helpful for further study. They have been grouped into categories.

SYSTEMS ANALYSIS

Books in this category examine the place of computers in library operations: needs analysis, purchasing equipment and software, managing a computer environment, staff training, and related topics. Some provide case studies.

Boss, Richard. *The Library Manager's Guide to Automation* (White Plains, NY: Knowledge Industry Publications, 1984).

Burton, P. *Microcomputers for Information Retrieval* (New York: Van Nostrand Reinhold, 1986).

Chen, C. *Microcomputers in Libraries* (New York: Neal-Schuman, 1982).

Corbin, John. *Directory of Automated Library Systems* (New York: Neal-Schuman, 1989).

Corbin, John. *Managing the Library Automation Project* (Phoenix: Oryx Press, 1985).

Costa, Betty. *A Micro Handbook for Small Libraries and Media Centers*. 2d. ed. (Littleton, CO: Libraries Unlimited, 1986).

Dyer, Hilary. *Human Aspects of Library Automation* (Gower, England: Gower, 1990).

Falk, H. *Personal Computers for Libraries* (Medford, NJ: Learned Information, 1985).

Genaway, David. *Integrated Online Library Systems: Principles, Planning, and Implementation* (White Plains, NY: Knowledge Industry Publications, 1984).

Intner, S. and J. Hannigan, eds., *The Library Microcomputer Environment: Management Issues* (Phoenix: Oryx Press, 1988).

Kesner, R. *Information Systems; A Strategic Approach to Planning and Implementation* (Chicago: American Library Association, 1988).

Kesner, R. and C. Jones. *Microcomputer Applications in Libraries* (Westport, CT: Greenwood, 1984).

Lane, Elizabeth. *Microcomputer Management and Maintenance for Libraries* (Westport, CT: Meckler, 1990).

Library Systems Evaluation Guides (Powell, OH: James Rush Associates, 8 vols. 1983-).

Matthews, J. *A Reader on Choosing an Automated Library System* (Chicago: American Library Association, 1983).

Rice, James. *Introduction to Library Automation* (Littleton, CO: Libraries Unlimited, 1984).

Walton, R. *Microcomputers: A Planning and Implementation Guide for Librarians and Information Professionals* (Phoenix: Oryx Press, 1983).

Two good non-library texts on systems analysis and development are:

Burch, J., Strater, F., and Grudnitski, G. *Information Systems; Theory and Practice.* 5th ed. (New York: Wiley, 1989).

Capron, H. L. *Systems Analysis and Design.* (Menlo Park, CA: Benjamin/Cummings, 1986).

DATABASE THEORY

Few books discuss database theory as it relates to microcomputers. The following give a good understanding of databases on mainframes, much of which is helpful in designing microcomputer databases.

Atre, S. *Database; Structured Techniques for Design, Performance, and Management.* 2nd ed. (New York: Wiley, 1988).

Freiling, M. *Understanding Database Management* (Sherman Oaks, CA: Alfred Publishing Co., 1982).

Gaydasch, A. *Effective Database Management* (Englewood Cliffs, NJ: Prentice Hall, 1988).

Kroenke, D. and Kathleen Dolan. *Database Processing; Fundamentals, Design, Implementation.* 3rd ed. (Chicago: Science Research Associates, 1988)

HARDWARE ORIENTED

These explain the parts of a computer, its peripherals and components, and how they connect. They give advice about buying computers and peripherals, and many discuss typical uses in libraries.

Melin, N., ed. *Essential Guide to the Library IBM PC*. (Westport, CT:
  Meckler, 1985- [several volumes]).
Woods, L. and Nolan Pope. *The Librarian's Guide to Microcomputer Technology and Applications* (Westport, CT: Greenwood Press, 1983).

A good non-library text on microcomputer hardware is: Robert T. Grauer and Paul K. Sugrue, *Microcomputer Applications* (New York: McGraw-Hill, 1987).

dBASE ORIENTED

There are dozens of how-to books on dBASE III+ and IV that provide detailed instructions on how to get the most from the program. A few representative ones are listed, including a few library-oriented books.

Beiser, K. *Essential Guide to dBASE III+ in Libraries* (Westport, CT:
  Meckler, 1987).
Beiser, K. *Essential Guide to dBASE IV in Libraries* (Westport, CT: Meckler,
  1990).
Byers, R. and L. Heimendinger. *Advanced dBASE IV*. (New York: Brady,
  1989).
Castro, L., Hanson, J., and Rettig, T. *Advanced Programmers Guide Featuring dBASE III Plus* (New York: McGraw Hill, 1986).
Chou, G. *dBASE III Plus Handbook*. 2d. ed. (Indianapolis: Que Books, 1986).
Hayman, Lynne. *101 Uses of dBASE in Libraries* (Westport, CT: Meckler,
  1990).
Jones, Edward. *dBASE IV Programmer's Reference Guide* (Indianapolis,
  Howard Sams, 1989).
Palmer, R. *dBase; An Introduction for Information Services* (Studio City, CA:
  Pacific Information Inc., 1984).
Prague, C. and J. Hammit. *dBASE IV Programming*. 2d. ed. (Blue Ridge
  Summit, PA: Tab Books, 1990).
Ross, S. *Understanding and Using dBASE III Plus*. (St. Paul: West Publishing, 1987).
Simpson, A. *Advanced Techniques in dBASE III Plus*. (San Francisco: Sybex,
  1986).
Using dBASE IV (Carmel, IN: Que Books, 1990).

The manuals for dBase III and IV are well written and instructional. The dBASE III+ manual is in two parts: *Learning dBase III Plus* and

Programming with dBase III Plus. The dBASE IV manual consists of one large notebook and 14 other booklets, ranging from beginning tutorials to advanced topics.

SOFTWARE DIRECTORIES

These are reviews and listings of library applications software.

Dewey, P. *101 Software Packages to Use in Your Library* (Chicago: American Library Association, 1987).
Dyer, H. and A. Gunson. *A Directory of Library and Information Retrieval Software for Microcomputers,* 4th ed. (Gower, England: Gower, 1990).
Mason, R. *Library Micro Consumer: MRC's Guide to Library Software* (Altanta: Metrics Research Corp., 1986).

Index

Note: Instructive textual and program examples of dBASE commands, command options, and functions are shown in caps. Not every occurrence is indexed.